CO-INCIDENTAL ENCOUNTERS

UNBEARABLE: BOOK ONE

T. XORÌ WILLIAMS

ISBN: 978-1-973925-64-4

For my one and only.

My best friend.

Mom, I love you.

ACKNOWLEDGMENTS

I would like to express my love and gratitude to the many people who saw me through writing this book; everyone who provided support, discussed topics, read, wrote, commented, allowed me to quote their remarks and assisted in the editing, and proofreading.

Above all, I want to thank my number one fan: my mother, my rock and my best friend. Your strength gives me courage. We've gone through many hardships. But you never complained or gave up. Instead, you learned to endure the hard times and raised your children to be just as humble as you are. I attribute all the success in my life to you. Thank you for always providing your never-ending support and encouragement. I have no clue where I'll be without your dedication. Please continue to be strong! I love you for my life!

My one and only savior, my God, thank you for seeing me through the best and worst times in my life. Continue to keep us all in your prayers.

To the rest of my family, I love you all.

To my twin brother B-Wise and Big Sister Tasha, who supported and encouraged me, y'all are my world. I love you both!

Thanks to my second brother Rah... AKA Dun Dun... We need you out here! We miss you! Thank you so much for all your work, support, editing, and saying "This book is dope, sis"!! OUR book is next!! Love you, Dunny!

I would like to thank my King for helping me in the process of selection, editing, and encouraging me to stay focused. It took us a while, but we did it! Your motivation and momentum have encouraged me ultimately. Thank you for showing me the true meaning of "there's never enough time in a day when you're working hard." We are building! Ningefanyaninibi-lawewe! Keep grinding! Love you most!

Karen, my second biggest fan! Thanks for being my supporter from the very beginning. I appreciate you!

Shayna, Shevonne, Robert, Amy, my APPS and EA family, ladies from Queens of Value, Angelica, Karen, and Donna--thank you guys so much for providing your feedback, support, and opinions. My 160 family, I love you all. Fat Sha and Uncle Wize (our angels), please continue watching over us. My editor Elaine M Foust.

Last but not least: I beg forgiveness of all those who have been with me over the years and whose names I have failed to mention." I love you all!

Enjoy!

PROLOGUE

For what it's worth, I never thought I would want someone with such dire urgency as I do right now; no symphony compares to what I'm feeling at this present time.

W aiting by the windowpane listening to Sade's "No Ordinary Love" in the dark for a man I've longed for weeks to be with. The high tide of the world has been keeping us apart, but thankfully that has subsided.

Repeatedly I've told myself I shouldn't be here; I should just walk away. But yet being with him in his arms feels just right. It's where I find my safe haven, my home away from home.

I am patiently waiting for him at the Trump Hotel in Manhattan's SoHo district.

SoHo is one of the most commonly known areas in New York City. The neighborhood is known for its artistic legacy, boutiques, and nightlife. We always wanted to try the hotel's luxury Hammams, Moroccan, Turkish spa treatment and head to the pool deck and have a cocktail in a private cabana. However, we can't enjoy the nightlife due to our unfortunate circumstances.

Even though we are unable to take pleasure in the hotel amenities, just being in each other's presence is quite all right.

I am staring outside New York City, and the sights are miraculous. I am surrounded by Manhattan's landmarks and historic sites such as the Hudson River, Midtown Manhattan, the Empire State Building, and the East River bridges. The sight is a wonderful blend of old and new; it is a delightful city, relaxed and fun.

I AM NOT much of an emotional person. However, waiting anxiously and nervously for this man, I just can't help myself. I am becoming increasingly emotional.

Hearing the thunder rumble and watching the raindrops fall, I press my forehead up against the window. Just the thought of soon to be lying beside this man marked by great beauty named Jayden Carter is nearly pushing me over the edge. Hmmm, I can feel his sweet kisses all over my body. For crying out loud, I smell this man in my dreams.

SUDDENLY, while in deep thought, I am startled by his muscled arms being wrapped around my waist. I inhale as if my life depended on it. He is here.

I slowly maneuver my head to the right, providing him with more room to kiss gently on my neck. My breathing pattern begins to deepen as I continue to endure his sweet kisses. I moan quietly.

This moment is endless.

I place my hand on the back of his neck and began to slowly gyrate on his manhood. He whispers in my ear in his raspy seductive voice, "How have you been,

Zadie?" Before I am able to answer, he turns me around, looking intensely into my eyes.

"I've missed you so much, baby."

"I've missed you just as much, Jayden."

"You look good tonight."

"I try. Thank you." I'm blushing as if I was a twelve-year-old schoolgirl. He always knows the right things to say.

"Well, you seem to do a phenomenal job for only trying."

I am gazing into his gorgeous brown eyes, which melt me completely.

He softly kisses my forehead and inhales deeply. As he removes my cashmere shawl, I wince as if I was in pain or distress. Without delay, he steps back, observes my bruised shoulder, clenches his jawbone, and sighs.

"Let me guess; he did this to you?"

"Jayden, I really don't wish to—"

He silences me by placing his finger over my lips.

"We don't have to talk about it. Don't say another word."

By his increased heart rate and respiration, I can tell he is agitated, but I completely understand.

He places his hand on my lower back, pulling me in close. We then indulge in a soft, passionate kiss while caressing each other amorously. His hand slowly moves up my back toward my shoulder, and I flinch again. Thank God, this time, he doesn't notice. I couldn't bear to see his displeased expression again.

I immediately grab his hand and guide him to the other end of the penthouse suite that is surrounded by open curtain floor-to-ceiling windows.

We are on the 40th floor overlooking the beautiful Hudson River, no one in sight but just the two of us.

While walking to the other end of the room, he stops abruptly, embracing me tightly, my back to his front, planting soft kisses on my nape. At this point, I can feel his full-fledged erection; oh my, I can taste him already. He unexpectedly let's go of me, and I stagger.

While he walks into the kitchen, I begin to wonder what he is going to do. But I continue walking to the other side of the suite yet again, gazing out the window.

He's behind me.

Upon his arrival, he places my hands on the window, gently holds my waist, and begins to place delicate kisses on my neck. He raises my black sundress, revealing my bare behind. He continues to kiss me, one kiss after another, passionately massaging my braless breasts, circling my nipples with his fingers.

I begin to pant.

Jayden removes his hand from teasing my breast, then inserts an ice cube into my mouth. Oh gosh! It is only ice, but holy cow, it tastes like heaven. Jayden then opens my legs by using his foot. He places an ice cube in his mouth, then down my lower back; the ice begins to melt down the crevice of my behind.

With force, he turns me around; now my back is to the window. He drops to his knees, places another ice cube into his mouth, grabs my hips, and thrusts both legs over his shoulders. Swirling the ice in between my thighs, I gently whisper, "I've missed you much."

I am now taking short, fast, shallow breaths, rubbing my hands vigorously through his hair. He teases my love box by gracefully blowing cold air on it from the ice that is melting delightfully in his mouth.

While he's kissing my inner thighs, I begin to shiver with anticipation.

Climbing back to his feet, he miraculously takes off my dress as well. My legs are shaky but planted back onto the floor.

He stands in front of me, searching my eyes. He grabs my chin and embraces me with a soft kiss, while his other hand skillfully plays with my kitten. My bottom lip begins to quiver, and I just can't take this anymore. "Jay, I need you inside of me."

Without hesitation, Jayden turns me around. But he doesn't cross the threshold just yet. He begins to massage and place tender kisses on my bruised shoulder. I close my eyes to relish this moment. Before I know it, he is inside of me, forcefully having me from behind. He quickly ejects himself from inside of me, turns me around, and then wraps my legs over his waist. Now we are kissing each other ever so hungrily.

He carries me over to the chair. I am now astride him, moving up and down, thrusting myself onto him. I see that he is beginning to tense by the vein in the center of his forehead. So, I began to smother his head in between my breasts, on my toes moving faster and faster, teasing the tip of his magic wand, and then back down the shaft. I do this repeatedly as I can't stop, then again, I really don't want to. Moments later, we climax simultaneously; we are breathless holding each other.

Then, out of nowhere, we start laughing like children. "I see we were eager," he says, still chuckling.

"Well, Jayden, it's been several long excruciating weeks. What did you expect?" We start to laugh again.

This is the moment that I love, the moment when we are away from our outside troubles embracing each other's laughter, love, and company. During my time with Jayden, I try not to think about life outside of him. I endure every moment spent with Jayden as if it's my last. Fairly often, the thought runs through my mind. The thought that Jayden Carter is the man I married.

CHAPTER ONE
SO, IT BEGINS

"I am only going to ask you this one more time, Zadie, where the fuck were you these last few nights?" he says, while he has her pinned to the floor in their living room with his foot planted on the back of her neck. Both of her arms are pulled behind her, and she is barely able to breathe.

The Beginning

Nazzir Baldamar, AKA Naz, two years ago at the age of thirty-three, Nazzir was a professional boxer. Boxing has been a part of Nazzir's life since childhood somewhere between sixteen and eighteen years of age.

Nazzir fought his first professional match at the age of nineteen. Even though it was hard to watch him fight, his wife Zadie says he was an exceptional fighter, and he made big bucks doing so.

Unfortunately for Nazzir, problems outside of work developed. His young sister Anna was involved with the wrong clique and began having personal problems with her boyfriend Clay. In the event, big brother Nazzir came to address the matter with Anna's obsessive and abusive boyfriend.

However, during their altercation, Clay unexpectedly larruped Nazzir across his head with a metal object, presumably a double hook car steering wheel lock, also known as "The Club." Nazzir immediately suffered a severe concussion.

Upon awakening, due to the blunt force trauma, Nazzir was unable to remember much about the incident. Even though he suffered from prolonged loss of consciousness, Nazzir was adamant about returning to his boxing career. Consequently, after weeks of being evaluated by healthcare professionals, the doctors announced that due to his injuries, his middleweight fighting career must come to an end.

He was torn apart, but thankfully, he has a computer engineering degree to fall back on.

Day in and day out at the hospital, week after week by his bedside, all Zadie could do was sit helplessly beside him, watching the love of her life dissipate. Unfortunately, since receiving the devastating news, Nazzir was slowly giving up.

She prayed that he would eventually come to his senses so they could go home. Weeks during the most unmemorable, unfavorable, injurious moments of their life, Nazzir finally found his strength, his will, and courage to survive; he didn't give up. They finally released him from the hospital with close monitoring, but they were on our way home!

After five years of being his lady, while leaving the hospital, he asked her to stop the wheelchair and to stand in front of him. He then gazed fixedly and intensely into her eyes as if his life depended on it; finally, he said he wanted nothing more than to spend his life with her

How We Started

Nazzir and Zadie met several years ago on the local New York City A train heading downtown. She was on her way to school, and he was going to see his sister. Nazzir really wasn't her type of guy. But on the other end, he was tall, muscular, and smelled pleasant.

She spotted him staring at her the first few times they crossed paths, but he never said a word. Then finally, after weeks of eye flirting, he approached her.

At that time, she wasn't looking for anything serious since she was about to start her residency at the local hospital. However, Nazzir and his charismatic personality convinced her otherwise. Since then, they have been inseparable.

When Nazzir asked to take her hand in marriage, she couldn't have been happier. But that was years ago; things just haven't been the same since his concussion...

CHAPTER TWO

SO, IT CONTINUES

As she begins to desperately gasp for air, he removes his foot from behind her neck.

"Please Naz, let me explain!"

He glares at her with fire, anger, and malevolence. "EXPLAIN?" He is laughing hysterically, and then abruptly switches back to his monotone voice. "Explain what, Zadie?"

Ok, it is official he is scaring the hell out of her. She begins to tremble uncontrollably.

"Will you explain what you were doing out there and with whom you were doing it? Will you explain that, Zadie?"

He grabs her by the neck, brings her to her feet in the process; she is being slammed up against the full-length mirror. It shatters on her back.

She can feel the glass lacerating her skin. Still being held by her throat, he kisses her roughly while salivating on her face.

"You clearly do not understand how much I love you!"

As much as she wanted to fight him, she just couldn't move from his tight, aggressive hold.

He is six feet three inches and two hundred forty pounds of pure muscle to her tiny figure of five feet four inches and one hundred fifty-eight pounds. She would be a damn fool even to attempt to make an antagonistic move, especially while he is in this state of mind.

"After all I've done for you, Zadie; you conniving, deceitful little bitch. Do you have any idea how much money, time, effort, and dedication I've put into you, into us? And to also mention into your Goddamn education, DO YOU!? You are the bright M.D. You should be able to figure out that question rather quickly."

At some point, she started to believe Nazzir was envious because she had a career going, and his career ended abruptly.

Okay, yes, he is right. The last few years, he paid for her schooling at NYU School of Medicine. It took her quite some time to complete, due to a few interruptions, but she is only twenty-nine and currently in her last few months of NYU Medical Residency program—thanks to him.

However, during her first few years of medical school, she hustled her tail off to make it through, from student loans to also paying out of pocket. She can't even begin to say how much money she put into her education. However, it was in fact, well worth it.

She was very grateful for Naz as he helped a substantial amount. He was an excellent provider during, and even after his boxing career; she honestly didn't know where she would be without him. Well, at least up until now.

"Nazzir you are overreacting; please just put me down and listen to what I have to say!" She was trying her best not to raise her voice and convince him to relax, but nothing was working!

"You want down bitch?"

He throws her back onto the floor. Broken glass yet again penetrates her skin. Then he drags her to the bathroom.

As odd as it sounds, the bathroom was her place to relax; weird, but it was. They had large light-colored wall tiles laid horizontally, as it made the room look larger. There was a freestanding bath, walk-in wet-room style shower, under-floor heating and a chaise seating area. They also built a wall aquarium to maximize relaxation with a built-in music system. It was always a great place to think, analyze, and to ease her mind.

"Stand up!" He commanded, and she complied, barely making it on her feet.

"Take off your clothes."

She was still wearing the same outfit from last night. For days Naz was patiently waiting for her arrival, and when Zadie arrived, she wasn't able to put her purse down, take off her shoes or grab a glass of water. He immediately dragged her inside the house!

"Nazzir, I am exhausted. I've been doing my residency for the past several days. Please, can we just put this behind us and go to bed?"

She attempted to rub his face, but he immediately grabbed her hand and bent her fingers backwards.

"OMG Nazzir, you are fucking hurting me; stop this please!" She nearly fell weak to her knees, but he pulled her right back up.

"Don't fucking touch me, Zadie, do you understand? Now take off your goddamn clothes!"

She started to take each item off slowly one by one, uncomfortably staring at Nazzir. This is her damn husband, yet she feels so violated! She doesn't understand his point in any of this, not one bit! What in the world is he going to do?

Her shirt was the first item she placed on the sink; then she attempted to place her brassiere there as well. However, this time he doesn't allow her to; he grabbed and held her bra in one hand and her pants in the other. She stood there in her panties, awaiting further instructions. A hot stinging sensation came across her.

"Fuck, Nazzir!" she yelled. His enormous hand gave her one good slap across the face.

"Don't fucking play stupid; take off your damn panties, Zadie, or next time I will knock the shit out of you. Do you see a dunce cap on my head?"

"No Nazzir, I don't see a dunce cap. You are a very smart man, and that is what I love about you the most. Baby, can we stop all of this and just talk please?"

SLAP across her face again.

"Don't dare patronize me, bitch."

In the process of pulling her panties down, he yanked them off. Then he immediately took a whiff of them. Thankfully she took a shower prior to leaving the hotel.

He is just standing there, staring her up and down.

"Sit on the edge of the tub, Zadie."

He got on his knees, abruptly opened her legs to smell her kitten.

"You think you are slick, huh. How is it that you smell fresh, Zadie!?" he roughly stuck his finger inside of her. Then he immediately thrusts her body into the tub, rips down the shower curtain, wraps her body tightly in it like some damn kind of cocoon; thankfully as of this point, she can breathe since he was kind enough to leave out her head.

He began to pace the bathroom floor; "You must think I'm brainless, you must think I'm fucking stupid, Zadie."

While pacing, he pulls out his 9MM from his waistline.

"I should kill you right here, right now." Then he placed the same finger to her nose that he placed inside of her. "You smell that shit right there, that is pure guilt, Zadie, pure fucking guilt. How could you do this to me? How?"

All that she could do was stare at Nazzir in complete awe. He abused her often, but she's never seen him this upset. She didn't know what to say. She was in awe, praying to God to get out of this alive.

"Answer me, Zadie!" It was becoming harder to breathe; the shower curtain was wrapped around her so tight. Her arms were so close to her chest that she was beginning to lose oxygen.

"Answer me, Zadie!"

As much as she wanted to answer, she couldn't. Zadie lacked brightness, vividness, clearness, and strength.

"Zadie, I said…"

She fell into a state of unconsciousness.

CHAPTER THREE

JAY

12:50 pm on Zadie's cell phone:

"Hey, guys, you reached Zadie; please leave me a message: Hey jungle toes, it's Jay. I haven't heard from you. Give me a call. Peace."

5:45 pm,

"Hey, guys, you reached Zadie; please leave me a message: It's Jay again for the um-some time... I'm getting worried sugarplum; You should've gone to your house with police escort. It's been a while since I heard from you; please give me a call, text, something, anything. Peace."

~

"WHAT'S GOOD, Jay, the patron would like to thank you for the great meal selection during their banquet.

"Jay, did you hear me?"

He was clearly in a daze.

"Yes, Cliff, I heard you, sorry about that kid, I will be out there in a few."

"Is everything ok?"

"Yeah, I am straight Cliff. Are you alright?" Jay asked jokingly.

"Yeah, I am doing alright myself—just tired."

"Well, we just had a huge banquet for the commissioner; I can only imagine how tired you guys are. Once we move out, our guests, you, and the staff can go home early. I will hire additional workers for the cleanup process."

"That sounds great. Now Jay, get out there and show your face; you don't want to leave our guests waiting now, do you?"

Cliff and Jay have been cool since grade school; Jay considered Cliff his little brother. He is also one of Jay's best floor managers at the restaurant.

The banquet was just about over; the team's services were appreciated for the lavish meal and prompt service. They did have a hectic day, so Jay allowed his employees to go home early. In the event, he should be going home himself. But he decided to take a drive to the Hamptons. Not hearing from Zadie was really ticking his nerves.

2 Hours Later

Jay made it to the Hamptons, and parked three cars down from Zadie's home. Noticing her 430i BMW and his 740i BMW confirmed they were both home. His blood began to boil. He and Zadie had been talking about stopping the affair, but she's not the type that would just ignore him like this.

They were too cool and close for her to just drop him like a damn bad habit. Unless--while rubbing the hairs on his chin—unless he... Nah, he really doesn't want to think anything negative happened... He turned off his engine, rested his head on the seat to figure out his next move.

Zadie

Upon awakening, she realizes she is freezing, her toes are numb, and her fingers are wrinkled... Why is she still naked in this freezing cold bloody water?

She looks around. Thankfully, no one is present. While still in pain, she unwraps herself from the shower curtain and slowly climbs out of the tub, walks to the mirror to look at her lacerations. From what she can see, he really did a number on her back.

She grabs her shirt and pants that she placed on the sink; her undergarments are nowhere to be found. She slowly opens the bathroom door. The house is very dark and quiet, but the coast is clear. She's planned on leaving her husband for a very long time, and it looks like today is going to be that day.

Walking into the living room, she accidentally walks on shattered glass. She starts hopping on one leg like a kangaroo, with her hands covering her mouth, preventing her cries of pain from being exposed. Finally, she was able to calm herself down and take the piece of glass from her foot. She sighed with relief.

Suddenly she was startled by a noise coming from the other end of the room; it sounded like a manly cough.

She is trying her best to quickly hop across the floor to hide beside the oversized armoire.

As she positioned herself, she noticed a trail of blood from her bruised foot leading right to her location.

*"*FUCK!*"* She says that pretty loudly. Five, maybe ten minutes later, no one shows up. She reluctantly moves from my location praying nobody is waiting on the other side of the armoire. Phew, again, the coast is clear.

7:16 pm.

She struggles her way into the day room, where she left her purse. It is pitch black in this house, and she almost knocks over her vase. She silently maneuvers to prevent the vase from falling; *I should be one of Charlie's damn angels*, she thought.

Suddenly, she hears a hoarse sound coming from the right of her in the dayroom. She immediately spins around, startled by her husband sleeping upward on the sofa. She walks over to him, contemplating if she should go and get a knife. The closer she gets, she notices the gun by his side, half-dressed with an empty bottle of Tequila on the floor.

I should kill him! But as tempting as that sounds, she decides she is just going to walk away as the smarter person. However, she is in a little pickle... her purse is under his foot on the ottoman. *But come to think of it, fuck the purse, I'm out!* She runs to the door; tries to disarm the alarm; but the pass code doesn't work... she tries it again. *Don't tell me; please don't tell me, he changed the pass code!*

She knows the moment she opens the door, the alarm will trigger. He is so much better with these things than she is. She doesn't even know how many wrong attempts she has before it permanently locks and sounds the alarm. Maybe she should just make a run for it, but with her foot in the position that it's in, she doesn't think she will make it very far.

Maybe he's so drunk he wouldn't even wake up. *Don't panic, Zadie, don't panic. Think--think.* She holds her breath to hear if he is still snoring. *Thank God, he is. Maybe if I call the alarm company, they will automatically disarm the alarm.*

Nah, she doesn't think it is that easy; she is sure they'll need confirmation of some sort. What could he have possibly changed the code to? The last code was, of course, their anniversary. So, she tries his birthday; that isn't it. She tries her own birthday; that isn't it either.

"What the fuck do you think you are doing, Zadie, trying to leave me?"

She tries to make a run for it, but she slips, thanks to the blood that spews from the bottom of her foot. In the process of falling, she knocks over the same damn vase she saved earlier; how ironic. But that doesn't stop her; she knows he is drunk, so she takes full advantage.

He grabs Zadie by her hair, swings her to the floor; now she's swinging all of her limbs for dear life. She cut him in between his thighs with a piece of the vase she grabs while he is pulling her up.

She is able to release herself from his hold. She opens the door and runs out as fast as she can. Suddenly she stops. Since he's up, she should get her purse off the ottoman. She was sure at some point, she is going to need her ID. So, she runs back inside the house, kicks him in the groin to make sure he wouldn't be getting up anytime soon. She grabs her purse and sneakers; then she kicks him again and run out without even putting on her sneakers.

She is sure the authorities or neighbors will be at the house shortly, due to the sound of the alarm if he doesn't shut it off; but she doesn't care, she runs out of there. She runs as fast as she can with her bleeding foot, and once she makes it safely up the street, she grabs some napkins from her purse, wraps her foot, and then she puts on her sneakers.

They live in a very secluded area in the Hamptons. She walks several blocks to the nearest gas station/convenience store for a bottle of water and some bandages for her injured foot. Then she continues to walk another half hour to the storage facility

"Hello, how may I help you?" asked the young lady.

"Hi, yes, I lost my storage key, and I need to get my belongings out of my compartment," Zadie is sure the attendant can see she's distraught.

"No problem at all, can I have your first and last name please?"

"Sure, it's Zadie Baldamar," she said while forcing a smile and looking out the window every second. She wishes to hurry things up already!

"Ok Mrs. Baldamar, It shows you have a rented unit in the basement, may I please have your ID?" She reached into her purse, pulled out her wallet.

"Here you go." As she opened the drawer full of keys, Zadie can see headlights from a distance.

"Here are your keys Ms. Baldamar." Not intentionally, but she rudely grabs the keys and her ID without even saying thank you, then ran to the door that led to the basement. But right before opening the door, the young lady yelled.

"Mrs. Baldamar, we must add the lost key fee to your account!"

She yelled back "That's perfectly fine!" Then down to the basement she went.

When entering the basement, she noticed numbers on the wall that'll guide her to the number that is on her key. She's only been here twice and can't remember in which direction her storage unit is located. She's only two numbers away.

Finally, she opens the door of the storage compartment; everything seems intact. A sigh of relief escapes. She starts the car that she had stashed inside the unit, just to make sure it's working. She hears the beautiful sound of a working engine! She pops open the trunk, where she stashed two big duffel bags. She takes both bags from the trunk and places them beside her on the back seat.

One of the bags includes a first aid kit. She immediately dresses the wound on the bottom of her foot with the proper ointment and bandages.

She realizes that she still had the storage doors open. She quickly gets out of the car to close the unit doors. Since she was unable to see, she turns on the car's headlights. Going back into the bag, she grabs her comb, brush, and ponytail holder, and tightly pins her hair back. She places a long brown wig with a cap on to disguise herself.

She knows that once he finds her, he will kill her. She must try her best to look discreet. Watching one of her favorite movies *Enough* really provided her with good ideas, and she clearly has had *enough*. She changed into something comfortable and finally put on some under-garments.

She placed some of the stored cash she had from one of the duffel bags into her wallet. Throughout the past few months to nearly a year, she had saved some cash. She wasn't one of those females that fell off her game because her husband was taking care of her.

Even though a lot of the money was from his allowance to her, she surely saved just about every dime. She jumps out of the back seat and into the front. She opens the glove compartment, takes out the prepaid phone along with a prepaid card to load minutes. Ok, now since that's done, she must call her sister Zamora.

Sisterly love

"Hey Sis!"

"Zadie?" Zamora asked.

"Yes."

"Where the hell have you been? And whose number is this? It's twelve midnight. I haven't heard from you all day."

She sounded so worried. "I know sis, I am very sorry, things just..."

"Things just what, Zadie? I've been so worried. Neither you nor Naz were answering the house and cell phones.

Something is going on; what's going on, and don't make me ask again."

Now she sounds upset! Zadie loves her sister with all her heart; Zamora is her best friend, her confidant, and her right-hand girl. *I'm so disappointed with myself for not telling her sooner.*

Zadie begins to cry.

"Baby Sis, please don't cry; talk to me, I'm here for you, you know that."

"My marriage has gone from bad to worse. Nazzir has been physically abusing me for nearly two years."

Zadie waits for her to respond, but she said nothing. So, she kept telling her story. "Ever since his concussion, something went strangely wrong."

"He just knew never to hit me where others will notice, which was the reason you were oblivious to what was happening." Zadie takes a deep breath; Zamora is still silent.

"Yesterday, when I came home, he was waiting for me."

When Zadie tells her that he tried to kill her, Zamora drops her phone.

"Zamora, I know you're upset because I..."

"UPSET is not even the word!" Zamora abruptly cut her off mid-conversation. "Zadie Julius, YOU HAVE NO IDEA!! I can spit flames right about now. This man has been abusing you for YEARS and Sis, he tried to kill you!?" She inhales deeply.

So Zadie tells her the whole story about what had just happened today—the *whole* story!

"Oh, how were you able to keep this from me, Zadie, as tight as our bond is? I tell you everything, and I thought you did the same too. I am beyond furious with you; he could've killed you because your ass decided to stay with him after all the shit he put you through."

"Tell me, Zadie, is he the reason you lost the baby several years ago? I swear—if you lie to me!"

Zadie never heard her sister this upset.

"Yes, Zamora, he pushed me out of his moving vehicle, but sis there's more." Silence on both ends of the receiver.

"I'm listening, Zadie."

"Well, since things were going downhill with Nazzir, I've been having affairs, and I've decided to leave finally. I really want to be with this guy, he is such an amazing man. I love him, and I really want you to meet him. He's a great man, Zamora."

"I know this all sounds crazy since I am married and all, but he is whom I want to be with. I also think Nazzir started to feel the distance between us, which is probably why he continued to abuse me. I feel it's entirely my fault."

"You know what Zadie; I was praying you wouldn't sound like the typical female and say some dumb shit like 'it was all my fault.'"

"This is exactly why I didn't want to tell you shit, Zamora! All you do is fucking judge me!" She lashed out.

"Zadie! You've been getting physically abused by your husband for damn near two years. Not a single woman deserves to be abused, regardless of what the situation is or what their man supposedly sensed. Mom and Pop are turning in their grave right now. You are so much better than this. I could kill him!"

"Yeah, well, you and I both. I am done with him, Sis, I promise you that."

"I really pray that you *are* done with him, Sis. Are you still in the storage unit?"

"Yes, barely able to breathe, I need fresh air." Both of them chuckled.

"I bet you do. Come here and stay with me; don't worry about your clothes or anything just come to Queens."

"Sis, I need to get my life together, and I can't be shacked up with you. I will be fine, plus your home and work will be one of the places he'll come looking for me."

"Are you going to stay with this new guy?"

"No, but I will see him today and stop by to see you as well. Just keep this number stored, ok? I will keep in touch."

"Oh no, after what you just told me. I don't like this. I will not be able to sleep, not knowing where you're going! That is completely out of the question, Zadie!"

"Zamora, how can I tell you where I am going if I don't know myself? I can't go to my residency, we both know that'll be the first place he'll check. I have a cell and you can reach me anytime. I am sure he will reach out to you soon, or come knocking on your door. So, as much as I want to stay with you, I can't. I love you, Sis; I will be fine, don't worry too much about me, ok?"

"I really hate this, Zadie; worrying about you is something I do at all times. I don't feel comfortable about this at all."

They are both silent for a few seconds.

"But, I must accept that you are smart, and you've learned from your mistakes, correct?"

"Yes, Sis I have. Let me get on the road; I'm suffocating in here."

"You need to take care of those lacerations on your back, and the cut on your foot. Ok?"

"I will try Sis; I will talk to you later. I love you."

"I love you most, Zadie; please be careful."

I quickly disconnected the call. I didn't want her to hear that I was getting emotional again. I got out of the car, slowly opened the gate, made sure the coast was clear, and so it seemed. I got back into the car and pulled out of the oversized storage unit, went to close the gate, and on the road I went.

Reminiscing

Driving through the streets of South Hampton, many thoughts were running through Zadie's mind. Moments like this are when she misses her parents the most. She was such a daddy's girl. Her father was her inspiration. He assisted tremendously with her future and career path.

Pop always told her if she wanted to be like him, she had to work hard for it. She remembered many nights Pop came home from work; he would tell Zadie all the horrific, but yet terrific, stories of being a medical doctor. But none of his stories ever startled her. She wanted to be so much like him; even the scary stories were intriguing. She misses him so much.

One morning in 1995, she woke up to screams coming from Mom and Pop's wing of the house. On the top of her lungs, Mom yelled to Daddy, "Tim, get the bucket of water, are you able to get to the fire extinguisher?"

Daddy was choking and barely able to utter a word. Zamora and Zadie opened their bedroom door to see what was happening.

"Girls, get back into your bedroom and get into the safe-room, NOW!" Daddy yelled.

Daddy was so overprotective of his family that he reinforced his daughters' second closet into a safe room. They ran into the safe room, and by this point, they were unable to hear and see anything.

Just about an hour later, we heard a gentleman's voice over the intercom of the safe room.

"Is anyone in there?"

Zamora opened the door; there stood a fireman holding fire blankets. He promptly placed the blankets over their heads and led them out of the house.

All Zadie remembered was screaming for Mom and Pop, but no answer. Unfortunately, their mother and father did not make it. They died at the scene due to smoke inhalation.

After the deaths of their parents, their mother's sister Joanne took custody of Zadie and Zamora. From that point, Zadie followed her father's only wish, which was, if Zadie wants to be an amazing MD like him, she had to work for it—and that she did.

As far as her sister Zamora, she was inspired by our Aunt Joanne.

Joanne was a dance teacher, and a phenomenal teacher at that, till her unfortunate car accident. However, Zamora followed in her footsteps and became a dance instructor at a prominent dance studio in NYC, "Steps on Broadway," for many years. Then she opened her own dance studio nearby to where she resides. She dances like an angel. It seemed as if she was born to do just that.

Two hours later, Zadie made it to Queens in one piece.

CHAPTER FOUR

ZAMORA

72 Hours Later

"One, two, and three tulip, swirl, dip... Don't forget to swirl the leg up, behind the cast back down, and plie. Good job, girls. Take ten, hey, hey! Have water, not soda little ladies." There was laughter —outburst by Zamora's teenage ballet class.

Dancing provides relief to Zamora's soul. The art of ballet is breathtaking and magical; it is known for its grace, charm, class, and elegance. When Zamora dances, nothing seems to matter, and the world around her is mute, she dances for gratification.

Admiring Aunt Joanne had a major impact on Zamora's life. Joanne was a ballet choreographer for 15 years, and she possessed the highest degree of creativity. Watching her was an extraordinary learning process for Zamora since she was eight years of age. Then after a few years, dancing became an element Zamora loved passionately. Then eventually, she developed her own distinctive style.

"Miss Zamora."

"Yes, Trinity?"

"Has my dancing improved since our last discussion with my mother?"

"Trinity, did we have another meeting since?"

"No, Miss Zamora."

"Well then, there's your answer, Trinity." Trinity ambushed her with a huge hug, nearly pushing Zamora to the ground.

"Thank you so much, Miss Zamora!"

The smiles on her girls' faces make her day, every day.

Yet in hindsight, she often ponders about her sister, praying she's doing just fine. She actually came into work today, trying to forget about what occurred, but it's so hard. The thought of informing the authorities crossed her mind, but she couldn't bear putting her sister in any more harm. She hopes that Naz doesn't come to her studio or her home. She hopes Zadie is okay.

"All right, girls stop the chit-chatting and get back onto the dance floor."

Meanwhile

The telephone rings at Detective Xavier's residence.

In his sleepy raspy voice, "This better be a beautiful lady calling me at two in the morning."

"DETECTIVE XAVIER, I know it's crack ass in the morning, but I think you need to get down here and see this," Detective Scott says with seriousness in his voice,

"WHERE?"

"DOWN by the old swamp and snake road, off of Brook Boulevard."

"On my way."

Detective Xavier came to the New York Crime Scene Unit (CSU) as a part of the NYPD. He is responsible for processing crime scenes, forensic investigations of homicide, prevention and solving crimes, as well as other cases deemed necessary.

He is the reason NYPD is known by its nickname "New York's Finest." Xavier was recruited, and he passed the qualifying tests to join the force with excellence.

He worked effortlessly and provided dedication as well as commitment since his first day on the job. But as great as his life panned out, he had a few rough patches. Several years ago, not too long after Xavier made it into the force; his father died at Allen Hospital. His father was injured from a mishap that occurred on a construction site.

Xavier's father was his icon, his shadow, and his motivator. He loved his father immensely. When Xavier's father passed during his operation, Xavier blamed everyone from the doctors to even his own mother. And to this day, years later, he still has resentment towards his mother for bringing his father to that hospital.

"Good morning, Xavier."

"It really isn't a good morning, Scott."

Det. Scott and Xavier have been partners for about eight months. By surprise, they get along very well, as it is quite possible to get stuck with a jerk of a police partner. These two had the same style of policing and interest.

"No, especially for our victim."

"What do we have here?" asks Det. Xavier. Crime scene investigators uncover the body.

"Damn, I believe I know the victim," says Det. Xavier.

"The killing was pretty horrific."

"How?"

"Massive numbers of stab wounds; we counted forty-three, with at least six various types of knives. This is complete overkill and a clear sign that this was premeditated."

"Any sign of a struggle?"

"Yes, as you can see, our victim has many defense wounds, here and here." Det. Scott points to the victim's arms and hands.

"Thank you, Det. You can cover the body now," says Det. Xavier.

"Do you want to reach out to the victim's family?"

"No, not just yet."

Jay

Jay returns to the house after he drove two blocks to a convenience store to get a cup of hot coffee. *Should I sit in this car for another four hours calling her? I sure don't want to knock on the door knowing that he's home. Why hasn't she returned any of my calls?*

While still sitting in his car, Jayden notices Nazzir getting into a taxi cab. *I wonder where he's going.* As Jayden ponders, he finds himself at Zadie's front door. Jayden knocks to no answer; walks to the back door yet again, no answer.

Jayden peers through the front entrance window. He notices there was some kind of disturbance. Then Jayden sees what appears to be blood on the floor near the entryway. He begins to panic, takes his phone out to call the authorities, but stops. He dials her number once more, to no availability. "Hi, you reached Zadie…"

"Please return my call; it's very important!" he shouts to the phone.

He places the phone back in his pocket, rushes to his car, and then speeds off in a frantic state. While driving, he realizes he is going well over the speed limit and in complete disarray. He decides to pull over on the I-495 to gather his thoughts, as he attempts to call her number one more time.

Back To Zamora

"Goodnight, little ladies, have a great weekend. I'll see you Tuesday. I am sure you will see each other over the weekend, and if so, please practice your routine. Practice makes perfect ladies."

"Goodnight, Miss. Zamora!" yelled the girls as they left the dance studio.

Zamora was finally able to sit and relax after such a long drained-out weekend. Zamora dialed her sister.

"Hi, you reached Zadie, please leave me a message…."

"Hey, sis, I have tried both numbers simultaneously to no answer. I'm worried; please give me a call back.

While in the process of disconnecting the call, she immediately receives a call from an unknown caller.

I hate answering block numbers—this must be Zadie. "Hello, this is Zamora, how may I help you?"

No one answers...

"Hello, this is Zamora, how may I help you?"

Zamora is alarmed by the knock on the studio door. *What in the world is going on here?* She disconnects the call and walks to the door. She thought that one of her girls may have left something behind.

"What did you leave this time, Holly," Zamora says while opening the door to find out it is Detectives Xavier and Scott.

"Good evening, your name is Zamora Julius, correct?" asks Det. Xavier

"You have a good memory, Detective; my carjacking incident was nearly three years ago; anyway, how may I help you?"

"If my memory serves me right, your sister's name is Zadie?"

"Yes, what seems to be the issue, officer; did something happen? Is something wrong with Zadie? Please tell me this is not about my baby sister!"

The expression on Detective Xavier's face says it all. "I'm sorry, ma'am, there is no better way to say this, but based on the identification, your sister was found...

And before Det. Xavier could finish his sentence, Zamora drops face down to the ground.

CHAPTER FIVE

REALITY

J ay made it to Queens despite the situation looming over his head. He decides the best thing to do is to drive to his restaurant and work. He is sure work will help him clear his mind.

Jay enters the restaurant, and before saying hello to his employces; he rushes into his office where he checks his voicemail; but nothing from Zadie.

"What's up, Jay, you cool man?" asks Cliff.

Jayden never discusses his personal matters with his employees. However, Cliff is like a brother to him and can read his obvious frustration as clear as day. Since Jayden does not have anyone else to discuss this matter with, he decides to let Cliff in on what he saw at Zadie's house.

"Cliff, anything we discuss stays between us, right?"

"Man, Jay, you can't be serious?"

"Actually, yeah, I am dead serious."

"Listen, Jay; I have told you quite an array of stories about my personal life that I have trusted you with. You can trust me the same way."

"Well, it's like this, Cliff. I have been dealing with this woman, well, a married woman. We met here at the restaurant, and initially, we thought it wasn't going to be anything serious due to our situation, but feelings started to grow. Then two years ago, after her husband was seriously injured, he started abusing her just about every chance he got. She planned to leave him, not because of me, but because of the obvious."

"We would sneak into different hotels on the Upper West Side for hours, several times each month. But I tell you this; those few hours we spent together meant everything, the only thing that mattered was her. When we were together, the stress of the world was behind us, and our lives were at peace.... Feel me?"

"Damn bro, even if I wanted to, I couldn't look down on you. Shit happens. But for some reason, that's not what your attitude seems to be about right now. Did she break shit off with you?"

"Well, we just saw each other a few days ago, and I haven't heard from her since. Usually, when we part from each other, she'll sneak a text or an email advising me that she's good, but I never received that text or email. I mean, we spoke of calling it quits a few months ago, but I didn't think she would dismiss me just like that; it doesn't seem like something she'd do. I drove by their house today. I saw her car as well as the husband's in the driveway, so I assume she's good. But when I check back, her car is gone and I see him get into a taxi. So I walked to the front door, I looked in the window, and it appeared as if some type of confrontation happened at the front door.

I noticed shattered glass and what looked like blood on the floor. Then while standing outside of her house, I decided to call her again, just to see if maybe I could hear her phone ring from inside the house. However, I was unable to detect any ringtones. I am concerned and have no way of reaching her."

"Damn, that is a lot to take in bro. Do you, by any chance, know where she works?"

"Yeah, but due to her situation, I just can't roll up at her job and ask for her."

"How about you go to her job as a cousin, or buy flowers and pretend that you are the delivery guy. I am sure there are many ways we can figure out how to get into her job without anybody thinking anything suspicious."

"Yea, I guess you are right; I didn't think about all that, but most of the time, she's in school. She works only part-time. Her husband is the primary bread winner, since her focus was to complete her medical degree. I really hope she's all right; she has everything going for her.

One thing that I do remember: she has an older sister who is a dancer. I believe she e-mailed her information to me a while ago. I'm sure I can go into my archives and reach out to her sister, but damn, what do I say, how do I even approach her? Maybe I can pose as if I were a coworker or a classmate. But truth be told, I was just a secret side dude that no one knew about. Now here I am lurking and looking for a married woman I may be falling in love with."

"Nah, I feel you, Jay. But, just tell the sis that you are a friend seeking information on another friend, it's that simple bro."

"Yeah, I guess you are right. Well, here's the email, it has her address listed."

"Seriously, that's what's up. Let's go then!"

"Are you sure, Cliff? Do you think this is the right thing to do?"

"Yeah, I'm sure Jay; I'll drive…"

Back to Zamora

Det. Xavier placed Zamora on her back, elevated her legs, and wiped her forehead with a damp cloth that was found in the lavatory. He loosened the top button of her shirt, and within twenty minutes, she regained consciousness.

"Ms. Zamora, can you hear me; are you okay, how do you feel?"

While still groggy and lying on the floor, she asks "Where is my sister, officer?"

"Are you okay? I would advise you not to get up; you just passed out."

"Detective, where is my sister?"

"Scott, let's help her onto that chair."

"Please tell me what happened to my sister."

As Det. Xavier inhaled rather deeply. "We need you to come down to the morgue to identify the body. We are not sure if it is your sister, but at this time, we need confirmation from a family member."

While in deep thought, she hears the Detective speaking, but only in the distance. "Miss Zamora, miss, can you hear me?"

Suddenly there is a knock at the door, Zamora immediately jumped up and ran to see who it is.

"This must be my sister, officers."

While opening the door she blurts "Zadie, baby, is that you?"

Jay and Cliff are now standing at the door.

"Oh, I'm sorry; I thought you were someone else. How many I help you?"

"Good evening, I'm sorry to have startled you. I'm also sorry to bother you. But by the looks of things, I am assuming you are Zamora, Zadie's sister, correct? You two look so much alike," Jay says.

"I'm sorry, not to be callous, but I am going through a situation right now, as you can see." Zamora points to the Detectives standing behind her.

"No, I completely understand; my name is Jayden and this is my boy, Cliff. Zadie and I are pretty close. We typically talk every day. However, it's been awhile since I've heard from her, and I am just concerned."

"Jayden and Cliff, please forgive me. Come in."

"Detective, this is Jayden and Cliff. They are friends of Zadie."

"You can call me Jay, and this is Cliff," he states to the Officers.

"Pleasure to meet you both," Xavier states.

"Excuse me, but Ms. Zamora; may we continue our conversation in private?"

"Sure, Detective. Please give us a second; we'll be right back." Zamora says to Jay and Cliff.

Zamora and Xavier walk to the back room.

"Ms. Zamora, are you available to come with us now to identify the body?"

"Yes, let me just grab a few things, and I will be right with you," Zamora states shakily as she walks into her office to grab her belongings.

"I am sorry, guys; we have to leave for a while. We have a situation that we must attend to." Zamora says to Cliff and Jay.

"I'm sorry, but is Zadie ok?"

Zamora looks back at the Detectives, then again at Jay.

"I am sorry, Jay, but we aren't sure."

"Zamora, I apologize, but what does that mean? You are not sure about what exactly? Is Zadie okay, did he do something to her?"

The Detective looked at Zamora in bewilderment; while Zamora stares at Jay in disbelief. The Detective approached Jay.

"Sir, who did something to Zadie?"

Zamora immediately intervenes... While staring at Jay, Zamora turns to the Detective. "Nothing Detective, he means nothing by that, I am ready to go."

The Detective looks at Zamora and Jayden knowing something suspicious is going on, but he decided to deal with that situation at a later time. His primary focus is to have Zamora identify the body.

"Detective, can you give us a second?" Zamora pulls Jay into the backroom, "How do you know my sister, do you guys go to school together?"

With a shallow embarrassed expression on his face, Jay hesitates to answer, but decides on being truthful.

"Your sister and I are a little more than just friends."

"I figured so, just by the concerned look on your face; I just knew something else was going on between the two of you. Several days ago, my sister told me she was having an affair and how Nazzir, her husband, was abusing her. So, yes, I am aware of who you are.

"She also stated she was going to leave him for you, and how she was going to link up with you that same day, that was the last time I heard from her."

"Generally, your sister and I will talk every day. I just assumed by her not reaching out, she decided to cut me off and work things out with her husband."

"No, that wasn't the case at all, Jay. You must be very special since she was planning to leave her husband for you."

"She is special to me as well. You have no idea, as hard as I fought not to fall in love with your sister, it was impossible. She's a remarkable person."

"I know she is; I am just taken aback that after all this time, my sister, and my best friend, did not tell me that her husband was abusing her. Jay, I have something to tell you, I'm going to be completely honest with you and I need you to remain as cordial and relaxed as possible. Because at this point, the officers really don't know what's going on; quite frankly, I don't know what's going on." She began to choke on her words. "The Detectives need me to identify a body."

"A body?" he whispers to Zamora.

"We are not sure yet."

Jay begins to pace.

"Please, I need you to relax, we are not sure."

"May I come with you to identify the body?"

"Sure, but only you can come. I'm sorry, I am sure he's a close friend. But this is a sensitive and very personal situation."

"I understand. But he's my driver. I didn't bring my car."

"How far do you live from here?"

"I live about twenty to thirty minutes from here; I am right downtown."

"Ok, I'll take you home once we are done, but we must go now."

They drive in silence, following the car ahead of them.

The Morgue

"Ms. Zamora, my name is Rebecca Stone. Please follow me."

Rebecca; is a grief counselor who helps individuals identify their possible deceased loved ones.

"Ms. Zamora, please understand I will be with you during the entire identification process... Are you ready to enter?"

"No, I am not; may I sit down for a moment."

"Sure, I'm right here if you need me."

Zamora takes a seat; Jay sits beside her. While grabbing her hands, "I'd love to hold your hand during the whole process, if you don't mind."

Zamora latches her hand to his and then nods in agreement. Both stand up and walk towards Rebecca.

"We are ready," says Zamora.

Rebecca leads us into a cold, stark, and dark morgue, with the deceased covered on the table. Rebecca slowly reveals the deceased's face for identification.

Zamora nods stoically, gasps in horror, then collapses into a fit of bawling, while the hardened police officers look on to her, and Jay stares at the body in disbelief.

Rebecca drops down beside Zamora to provide support and empathy. Rebecca allows Zamora to weep for several minutes; then Jay intervenes. Jay assists Zamora to her feet and then walks with her to the nearby sitting area. Zamora continues to cry on Jay's shoulder.

"She was all I had; she was my everything. Our parents died when we were so young. But we survived by each other's grace and prayer. I don't know what to do without her, Jay. I just don't. I'm so lost right now."

"If you are anything like your sister described, I know one thing, you are strong, Zamora. Your sister spoke highly of you; she loved and admired you dearly. She would need you to be strong at this time."

Zamora snaps. "That bastard did this; I know he did! I'm going to fucking kill him! While storming out of the morgue, Xavier immediately stops her.

"I understand you are hurt and scared. However, making irrational decisions would not solve a thing."

"Detective, her husband Nazzir Baldamar has been abusing my sister for several years. He has what I am sure is an unregistered firearm that he nearly forced down her throat several days ago. You need to check his ass, or I will!"

"Miss. Zamora, we will do our job. But you really need to take care of yourself."

"I need to go; please forgive me, Detective. I just need to get home, gather my thoughts, and try to get some sleep."

"That's a good idea. Please allow us to handle this. I promise, Scott and I will do all we can to bring the killer to justice."

Zamora is completely confused and shaken, mourning the death of her sister. Coming to the realization, she must now deal with her absence; accepting this loss is extremely challenging for Zamora. Her whole world collapsed within moments; she is terrified and alone.

"Thank you, Detective. Jay, I'm sorry I can't drive; can you please take me home?"

"Absolutely, I'll drive you home."

While Jay was driving to Zamora's house, she laid in the back seat of her car in profound thought.

Our relationship was the best. She was everything to me. If we went three days without speaking to each other, it felt like an eternity. I just can't wait to get my hands on that asshole; how could he do this, how could he do this to my baby sister?

Jay arrived at Zamora's home. Zamora lives about twenty minutes from her dance studio. Her home is in Sunnyside Queens, a small lovely private community that has a suburban middle-class feel. It overlooks the East River beautifully. You can almost feel the urge to reach out and touch the Empire State Building.

"Jay, I'm sorry to have taken you out of your way."

"Please don't worry about it. I'm glad to see you home safely."

"I know it's late, and I barely know you. But a friend of my sister is a friend of mine. You can stay in the guest room if you would like. I just can't be alone right now. I miss her so much, Jay. I just…"

As Zamora is in a deep sobbing state, Jay gets out of the driver's seat, enters the back with Zamora, and holds her tight as she cries.

Zamora says. "I knew something was off when I was unable to reach her."

"When did you last see your sister?"

"Almost a month ago, which is abnormal, but we made sure we talked every day."

"I haven't heard from her since the other night, which worried me and prompted me to look for you."

"My sister loved you, Jay. When she was talking about you even under distress, she was able to smile."

"I loved your sister dearly; I've always been disappointed that she was more interested in someone else other than me. We always had an amazing time together."

Zamora glanced at Jay with fury. "Another man?"

"Yes, I've been meaning to tell you, I just didn't know how to approach the topic. I really don't know much about him, but I knew she was dealing with him before she and I started kicking it."

"I just can't believe my sister never told me about you before the last time I spoke with her. Why keep so many secrets? She was an amazing young lady. I don't know what I am going to do without her. She loved others when they didn't even love themselves. She was full of life, such a bubble full of fun. Now look, she's dead from being battered by this jerk who claimed to have loved her.

She was dragged, beaten, and stomped on. HOW COULD HE DO THIS TO MY SISTER?!" Zamora became irate. She was hitting and kicking the back of the seat, like a toddler having a temper tantrum.

Jay took a leap of faith and grabbed Zamora's face.

"Look at me, Zamora! Everything that I've heard about you was great. One thing your sister repeated was how much of a mother symbol you became to her immediately after your parents died in that horrific fire."

"You took charge Zamora, and, as young as you were, you raised your little sister. You need to be strong for both of you."

"I know, but it is just easier said than done, Jay. But thank you. You seem to be such a nice guy and very kind-hearted. I can see why she fell for you."

"If you really need me to stay, I'll stay. If not, I'll walk you inside before calling an Uber.

"That'll be nice. Uber is usually here in less than ten minutes."

CHAPTER SIX

MORE DRAMA

As she opens the door, her place smells heavenly, with a mixture of fresh pine scent and vanilla incense. We were greeted with the smooth sound of Jazz singer Billie Holiday playing through her surround sound system. Her place is lovely; we enter a large foyer with polished wood floors, a sunken living room, the hallway flows into this large spiral staircase, along with a fireplace and cathedral ceilings.

"By the way, you have a lovely home."

"Thank you. I call myself the wannabe interior designer." We both laugh.

"Glad to know even during this hard time you're laughing; and for the record miss wannabe interior designer; you've outdone yourself."

"Thanks. Do you mind, I need to use the restroom? I'll be right back."

While Jay waits, he admires her place. Zamora's home is full of charm; it is stylish, peaceful, and relaxing.

Moments later, a loud scream comes from a room in the house. Jay runs around, looking for Zamora. He finds her on the floor in the bathroom, in a fetal position, crying. He carries her to the living room, supports her head on his lap while she wept. Nearly thirty minutes had gone by as she is trying to settle her own emotions, and all that she could say was "I miss her so much. This hurts so badly."

"I know, I don't have to leave, Zamora; I can stay, if you want me to."

"Thank you, Jay, but come to think of it, I should really be alone."

"You practically passed out in the bathroom, Zamora. I can stay; it's not an issue."

"I'm sure staying wouldn't be a problem for you. But I feel it is best that you leave. I need to gather my thoughts and get myself together."

"Okay. I understand. Please take my card, whenever you need me, I beg of you do not hesitate to call."

Uber arrived in only a few minutes after calling.

Just about an hour later, Jay arrives home.

Jay resides in a luxury apartment loft in Downtown Brooklyn, 389 Bridge Ave. His Loft has high ceilings; walls of windows, wide board oak floors, and a thoughtful blend of old and new, with a panoramic vista of nearly all of NYC landmarks.

"I can smell that bitch on you, why didn't you just stay with her? Why even come home, you scum bag!" Jay's wife Teri shouts.

"I am for sure not up to this shit tonight, Teri! We don't even sleep in the same God damn bed, sign the fucking divorce papers, and leave me the fuck alone. I just found out someone dear to me died; this is not what I want to come home to."

"I hope it's that bitch."

Jay looks at Teri with anger. Her acrimonious words drive him to pick his keys up and walk out.

"Have a good night" Jay slams the door behind him and drives into the night.

"Yo, Cliff, sorry man, I know it is late but can I crash at your place tonight?"

"You already know you can; you still have your spare keys?"

"Yea, be there in a few. Peace"

Before driving to Cliff's, Jay decided to head to his preferred location to relax and clear his mind, which is right outside of his loft. He goes to the Dumbo area directly across from the Brooklyn Bridge. Dumbo's spectacular waterfront view eases his mind every time. Jay shoots Cliff a text. I will be a little late, need to clear my mind.

While texting Cliff, Jay's wife calls.

"What is it, Teri?"

"Did I interrupt you while you're with the next bitch?"

Jay abruptly hangs up the call.

Moments later, another incoming call; Jay answers the line with haste.

"I don't need this shit right now Teri, how about you go fuck my brother again."

"I apologize, is this Jay?"

The distraught voice asks on the other end.

"Who is this?"

"Jay, it's Zamora; I'm sorry to bother you, did I catch you at the wrong time."

"No, Zamora, forgive me; I'm just having a bit of a rough night."

"Is everything ok?"

"I should be asking you that. So…... are you okay, Zamora?" Jay asks sternly.

"I thought I could manage this alone, but I can't. I don't want to inconvenience you, but…"

"I'm on my way, Zamora. I'll be there in thirty." He hung up the phone and began to drive.

BACK TO ZADIE'S HOUSE

"Hello, this is Detective Scott, and I am Detective Xavier, this area has been blocked off for investigation, how may we help you, Ma'am?"

"What happened here?"

"Ma'am, as you can see, this is a crime scene, and in order to maintain the integrity of the scene, law enforcement must take action to block off the surrounding area as well as keep track of who comes in and out to avoid contamination of the scene."

"Well, officer, this is my son Nazzir and daughter-in-law's home. Please tell me what's going on. It's been several days since I've heard from either of them, and I am worried."

"Ma'am, do you mind waiting here for a moment? Our responding officers are taking statements and wrapping things up. I'll be with you momentarily."

While forensics maintains the integrity of the scene, law enforcement must take action to block off the surrounding area. Forensics then uses a variety of different tools and techniques in collecting DNA and other bodily fluids. Documentation about the area in question is also taken for further research. The evidence has been collected from the scene of the crime and placed in its appropriate container, labeled or tagged.

- Initials and/or names of the person collecting the evidence, and all the subsequent people who have and will come in contact with the evidence

- The date of collection and transfer

- The name of the agency and type of crime

- Voucher or property clerk number

- The name of the victim or the suspect

- Where the item is being stored

- A summary of the items

"Ma'am, thank you for patiently waiting. Do you mind coming down to the precinct with us to answer a few questions?"

"Officer, please call me Nemea. But can someone tell me what is going on?"

"Ms. Nemea. We'll tell you everything you need to know. But we can only discuss this matter at the precinct."

Ms. Nemea agrees. She willingly enters the back of the officer's car to head down to the police department.

"Thank you for coming to the precinct with us; we really appreciate your time."

"Well, anything I can do, officer."

"Would you like something to drink, coffee, tea, soda?"

"Water would be nice."

"Scott, do you mind getting Ms. Nemea a bottle of water please."

"Can you tell me what this is all about?"

"Ms. Nemea, I'm awfully sorry to inform you, but your daughter-in-law Zadie was killed."

Her fear began to surface. Nemea screamed.

"THIS CAN'T BE! I just saw her! No, please, no. This can't be happening! Where is my son?"

"That's what we were wondering; you have no idea where your son might be?

"No, I don't! How dare you officer. If you're accusing my son, he would never do anything like this! He loved Zadie and would put his own life at risk for her"

"Ms. Nemea, we are just following proper protocol. As you've witnessed, there seems to have been a bit of a disturbance at the Baldamar's home."

"Detective....? Sorry, I am terrible with names."

"It's Detective Xavier, ma'am."

"My son loved his wife with his life! He would never, and I mean *never* do anything to harm her."

"When was the last time you heard from your son?"

"Well, officer, it's been a few days; hence why I went to his home."

"Do you, by any chance, know where he might be?"

"No officer, I do not know."

"Ms. Nemea, I think, those are all the questions we have for you at this time. Thank you so much for your cooperation. Here's my card; if you hear anything, Ms. Nemea, please don't hesitate to call."

Sunnyside

"Thanks for coming, Jay."

"The pleasure is mine." Jay walked into Zamora's living room.

"Wow look at this, what do we have here?" Jay asked.

"I'm gathering some photos of Zadie to make a blanket collage. I told her I would make it for her birthday this year. But while doing it, I just couldn't go on."

"How about we get something to drink, your kitchen is this way correct?"

"Yes, thank you, Jay.

"You got it. No worries at all."

Back to the living room, Jay and Zamora laughed and cried the whole night through, talking about Zadie and their childhood, till finally falling asleep on the couch.

"Good morning Jay, something smells great." Zamora says as she walks into the kitchen and sees Jay cooking breakfast.

"You didn't have to do this."

"Well, as drunk as you were last night, I figured you'd need a nice cup of recovering hangover coffee, and a full plate of pancakes, eggs, and sausage."

Both laughed while making their way into the dining room.

"This is amazing, Jay. Thank you so much; everything is just so delicious."

"You are more than welcome, Zamora. Well, I'll get out of your hair so you can get ready for work."

"No, I can't, Jay. I'm taking a few grievance days. I'm sure many would think work might be best, but at this point I just need time.

"Do… you…want me to stay with you?"

"No, I can't ask you to do that, Jay, you have a life to get back to."

Jay grabs Zamora's hand.

"Please understand; Zadie was a major part of my life. She was my home away from home. Being with you makes me feel close to her, if that makes sense."

"It makes perfect sense, all I have now are my girls; well, now and you, I hope."

"You are stuck with me now. I'll call my restaurant to make sure everything's running smoothly; I'll stay with you for as long as you need."

"Thank you so much, Jay."

She gave him a quick hug. "I can't thank you enough. Honestly, within the short time of knowing you, as crazy as it sounds, I am so thankful you came to my studio to look for Zadie.

"I am glad to be here with you. Zadie told me so much about you, so it practically feels like I know you. And we both loved her."

"I completely understand; it is an honor to meet you as well."

Jay phoned his restaurant.

"Is everything okay at the restaurant?"

"Yeah, everything is straight."

"Do you mind if I ask you, who is Teri? You mentioned her name in haste when I called yesterday?"

"No, I don't mind. Teri is my wife, pending divorce. We've been together for thirteen years, married for six.

"You are married too! What in the world is going on here! Everybody loves to have affairs! This is why I'm single! What happened between the two of you?"

"That's a long story, are you up for it?"

Zamora grabs her coffee, then takes Jay's arm and heads into the living room.

"I guess that means yes," Jay states.

CHAPTER SEVEN

GOT HIM

"Detective Xavier, we have word on the whereabouts of Nazzir."

"Where is he?"

"He's been seen at his professional boxing gym–in Brooklyn."

"Let's go," says Det. Xavier.

The detectives arrive at the boxing gymnasium and approach the owner.

"Good Morning, I am homicide Detective Xavier, and this is Detective Scott.

"How may I help you?"

"We are looking for Nazzir Baldamar. Do you know where he might be?"

"Officer, he is in the west wing of the gym."

"Thank you."

"Based on the description and pictures, I think that is him," says Det. Scott.

"Nazzir Baldamar?"

"Who is asking?" Nazzir turns around and notices two men dressed in nice suits.

"We need you to come with us?"

"For what?"

"Is your name Nazzir Baldamar?"

"Yeah."

"Ok then don't make this hard on yourself."

"I am not. I simply asked a question."

"Please come with us, Mr. Baldamar."

"Am I being arrested, officer?"

"Do you wish to cooperate with us or not?"

"I don't mind. Just tell me what this is all about."

"We need you to come down to the precinct with us; we have a few questions we need to ask you in private."

WHILE NAZZIR and the Detectives position themselves in the interrogation room, Nazzir asks, "Are you finally going to tell me what this is all about, Detective?"

"Would you like something to drink, coffee, water. Maybe a 9mm that you wish to shove down your wife's throat or a knife you wish to stab her with?" Det. Xavier asks sarcastically.

"What the fuck does that even mean, where is my wife?"

"Come on, Nazzir, I'm sure you killed her?"

Nazzir jumps out of his seat.

"My wife is dead! Don't fucking joke around like that officer! Zadie baby, come out from behind there, I am sorry. I will never put my hands on you again." Nazzir taps on the double-sided mirror.

"So, you admit to abusing your wife?"

"Yes, I was belligerently drunk and besides myself, I knew she was having an affair, so I flipped out. I went overboard, but what husband wouldn't. She was out there fucking around on me. I love her, and she knows that I love her more than life itself. Tell my wife to fucking come in here and drop any charges she filed against me; I love my wife."

"Sit and calm the fuck down." says Det. Scott.

"WHERE IS MY WIFE, YOU FUCKING PIGS?!"

"Listen here, you little dick of a jerk; I would hang you to dry. You fucking hear me?" Xavier whispers loudly while hovering over Naz's face.

"Give us a second, Mr. Baldamar."

While outside of the interrogation room, Scott grabs Xavier. "You need to calm down and get a hold of yourself. He seems to have no clue that his wife is dead."

"Yes, he fucking does; and take your hands off me! And don't ever pull a stunt like that again. Do not allow this dimwit to pull the wool over your eyes."

"You think he killed her, even after the reaction he just gave us?"

"Rookie, you are falling too soon into his trap. What you need to do when we go back in there is to not cut my fucking interrogation. I've been in this game for a very long time. Learn from me."

"What do you have against this guy?"

"Besides the fact that he killed his wife? Not a God-damned thing! Stop questioning me, amateur; watch, and learn. Let's go get lunch. Let this resonate for a while."

Back to Zamora's

"I CAN'T BELIEVE that you also go to the Dumbo area near the bridge to ease your mind; how odd," Jay said to Zamora.

"Yes, I go there just about every third day. I love that area."

"It sure is relaxing."

"I am sorry to bring this up, but seeing you get pretty emotional talking about your wife, I assume you must still love her."

"To tell you the truth, I do. But I can no longer be with her. It all just hurts so much by what she did."

"I am sure; I am still in shock. You guys were married for only two years, and she slept with your brother. That's huge. But then again, there are always two sides to every story."

"Zamora, prior to what she did, I gave her my all. She stayed home, didn't need to work because I took care of everything. I allowed her to have all she needed and wanted. We went to marriage counseling, support groups, and church. You name it; we did it. I couldn't get over it. Every time I was intimate with her, I saw his face. You have no idea how much that hurts... So, I told her I want a divorce, eight months later; I am still waiting for her to sign the papers. She refuses. Usually, the guilty party does."

"Well, I don't blame her, you're quite charming. Also, if you were spoiling me like that, I can guarantee you, I wouldn't divorce you either." Both laughed.

"You are quite an amazing person yourself, Zamora."

"Why, thank you. I see vividly as to why my sister admired you." While gazing into the eyes of one another, Zamora snapped out of it.

"So, what are you going to do, get a lawyer to help with the divorce proceedings?"

"I hired a lawyer just a few weeks ago; he is doing pretty well thus far. However, I am temporarily moving out until she leaves. I got myself a nice place not too far from my restaurant."

"Speaking of the restaurant, you are a chef, huh?"

"Yes ma'am; right after high school, I went to the Culinary Institute, graduated, worked at a restaurant as the dishwasher, read cookbooks, and watched cooking shows. Two years in and out of entry-level positions, I explored further advancement; I studied Italian and French, then I worked my tail off to open my restaurant. Seven years later, here I am, *Jay's Garnish* is the name of my restaurant."

"It's such an amazing story!"

"Hey, don't sell yourself short, miss phenomenal dance teacher. Tell me more."

"My story isn't as amazing as yours; my aunt that obtained custody of Zadie and me was an incredible dancer. I used to watch her dance day in and day out. So, I decided to become a Dance Instructor. I obtained employment at a dance studio in Manhattan, "Steps on Broadway," for many years. Then I decided to open my own dance studio, currently looking for a bigger location. It didn't take much to do it. But I will say this, sometime in the future; I will stop by your restaurant."

"Please do so. I'll be delighted to have you. Also, your story is just as amazing! One of these days, of course, under different circumstances, I will stop by the dance studio to take a look at your moves. But please come to the restaurant. You will love it. The invitation is always open."

"THANK YOU; I will take you up on that offer. Wait, did you say Jay's Garnish? I went there a few weeks ago with Zadie, were you guys dating then?"

"OH YEAH, that is right! She was there with her friend and Zadie told me I just missed you. No, we were not dating at that time. She only contacted me to do catering for a repast."

. . .

"THIS IS CREEPY. The repast was for someone very dear to me."

"SORRY FOR YOUR LOSS. This is such a small world. I have an idea, how about lunch today. You barely finished your breakfast."

"HONESTLY, Jay, I am physically here with you, and might I add, enjoying your company. But, I am breaking down inside; reminding myself that I have to bury my baby sister in the next few..."

Zamora begins to choke; trying to fight back the tears, but she couldn't fight much longer.

Jay moves closer to Zamora, but she quickly stands up.

"Jay, I am so sorry; you should go."

Jay stands up as well, grabs Zamora's hand.

"Stop doing this Zamora, why are you fighting me?"

"Fighting what exactly, Jay?" She releases herself from his grip.

"Zamora, we both lost someone very dear to us. I am not in any way trying to do anything unethical. I'm a friend trying to console another during this hard time. And to add, it is extremely disappointing and insulting that you would think of me in that way. As if I want something more from you. But, you know what, come to think of it, you're right; I'll go. Thanks for your hospitality."

Jay angrily leaves the house, slamming Zamora's front door.

"Jay, Wait!"

Zamora runs to the door to catch Jay before zooming off in his car.

"What is it, Zamora?"

"You said something yesterday that caught my attention. You said my sister was seeing someone else."

"Yes, she was seeing someone that she was going to leave her husband for."

"I thought that person was you."

"I believe their relationship was going on way before ours; I guess she loved us both. Have a good afternoon Zamora."

"Jay, wait, please. Do you by chance know anything about him?"

"Why would I? I was falling in love with your sister. I didn't care about him. So, to answer your question, no, I know nothing about that guy.

"Jay, I am sorry. Can you please come back inside?"

"Not, right now. I am a tad bit bothered. Maybe I'll be back later, if you don't mind."

"No, I don't mind at all."

Zamora goes back inside, leans her back up against the door, and slides down onto the floor, knees to chest as she begins to cry hysterically.

Back to Work

"Hey, Cliff, how's everything going?" asks Jay as he makes his way through the restaurant, and into his office.

"Everything is good, Jay. Maria and Lance called out, so we are short-staffed. How about you, how are you doing, what's going on with the case?" Cliff asks, following Jay into his office.

"Thanks for taking care of everything during this time, Cliff. Truth be told, I don't even know what is going on with the case; I am dead tired. Teri is working on my last nerve. I got so much shit to do right now; and I don't even know where to begin."

"I got an idea." Cliff heads to the bar.

"Here, Jay, kickback; let's have a drink and chill for a few minutes. Maybe this will help you stop bitching." Both laughed as Cliff handed Jay a snifter of Hennessy Cognac.

"Thanks, Cliff I need this. How are your Mom, Pop, and sisters doing?"

"Everyone is good, thanks for asking. But you, on the other hand, need to take a step back and relax. Oh shit, I forgot to tell you, guess who I ran into the other day?"

"Who might that be?"

"Remember skinny-ass Tara, from college? She is thick as hell now!"

"No way! I've got to see her. The chicks these days are doing too much to their bodies: ass shots, breast shots, probably thigh shots too."

Laughter again is shared between the two.

WHILE JAY AND CLIFF REMINISCE, Zamora heads to her sister's residence. She packs all of Zadie's belongings, informs her peers, coworkers, and acquaintances of the funeral, date, time, and place.

When Zamora gets home, she looks for any information in regard to this other guy Zadie was having an affair with. Then out comes Zadie's daybook. Zamora starts her bath, hops in the tub with a bottle of wine and a glass, and opens the daybook, and begins to read.

WHILE RE-ENTERING THE PRECINCT, the detectives receive the DNA results. The results prove that both Nazzir's and Zadie's blood was at the scene. They now have enough evidence to arrest Nazzir Baldamar for the murder of his wife.

Back into the interrogation room, they pry incessantly for hours but get nowhere with Nazzir. After Nazzir is drilled into finally believing his wife had been killed, he was in shock and began acting irate. Nazzir is then handcuffed to the chair after the Det. showed him the pictures of his deceased wife.

"Officer, if you are accusing me of killing my wife, I request my lawyer."

"We'll get you your lawyer, and we are charging you for the murder of Zadie Baldamar."

Det. Xavier phoned Zamora.

"Ms. Zamora, this is detective Xavier calling; we have detained and charged Mr. Nazzir with the murder of your sister. We have enough probable cause and physical evidence. Also we left your residence moments ago; we noticed your car out front. However, we were unable to reach you; maybe you were sleeping. Nevertheless, please return my call."

CHAPTER EIGHT
BREAKING BREAD

"Cliff, we've been drinking for a while; I should fire your ass for drinking on the job!"

"Whatever, man!" Cliff says, playfully shoving Jay.

"So, what are you going to do about Shorty?"

"Get off my case!" Jay said jokingly.

"Naw, I am dead serious."

"Cliff, how do I look approaching her; mind you, I was dating her married sister who just died. I look terrible in her eyes. Oh, and to also add, I too am married. Did you forget about that?"

"Yea, okay, you are right about that, but you served your wife divorce papers, and at this point, you are Shorty's Knight in Shining Armor. You two need each other right now; I am sure she needs you more because she has nobody."

"Cliff, you can't be that cold, are you suggesting I take advantage of her at this moment in her life?"

"Yeah, Jay! Straight like that. Think of it like this; she is vulnerable, which means she only needs love. That is where you come in."

"That is completely beneath me, you know that isn't how I move; my heart isn't as cold as yours."

"You just met her, though. What, you falling in love with the chick already?"

"Nah, I am not Cliff, but you wouldn't get it anyway. You are thirty-three and still need to grow up."

"Ahh, come on; the man doesn't throw jabs."

"This conversation is over; I am heading out, tidy up, close up, and stop drinking Cliff," Jay says as he walks out of his office.

"You're mad Jay--you know I'm only playing with you, man; cut it out."

Jay turns back to Cliff. "Nah, you are not playing, as you say, you are dead serious. But it is cool, Cliff, one thing about us; we stay out of each other's affairs. Until you find love, a good strong, educated, morally correct woman that loves and respects her mother, holds her own, and enjoys life--you will always be stuck playing too much." Jay walks out.

Just in Time

As Jay returns to Zamora's home, he notices her front door is ajar. Jay knocks before entering; he calls for her, but no answer. He enters the home. He notices what seems to be water pouring from the second level. He rapidly sprints upstairs, yelling for Zamora. He enters the bathroom where he finds Zamora, in the freezing cold tub with pills, Zadie's datebook, and a bottle of wine beside her while the water is overflowing.

Jay turns the water off, and then checks for a pulse.

"Thank God she is alive." He wakes Zamora by softly patting her face.

"Z, can you hear me?" As she opens her eyes, she moans.

"Jay, is that you?" Zamora asks with her cracked voice.

Jay immediately runs to grab a towel from behind the bathroom door. He wraps the towel around her cold body, carries her to the bedroom, positions her on the bed, and then he covers her in between the sheets. He lies beside her while she sleeps. Jay, managed to stop the leak and cleaned up the mess. Prior to leaving he places a bottle of water on her bedside table.

Two Days before the Funeral

"Alissa, table seven needs their meal, with extra parmesan, quickly."

"Sure, Jay, no problem. I am on it. Thanks," says Alissa.

"Yo, Jay. Isn't that the ol' girl standing over there?" Cliff points near the entrance.

Jay looks out through the kitchen door window, and he notices Zamora. Stunningly beautiful, the dress is flawless; it hugs her body gracefully, showing her curves as if the dress was made just for Zamora. It is topped with a dark brown lace bolero that matches her silhouette, as her hair hangs perfectly.

"Jay! Snap out of it! Go greet her before she leaves, or someone else takes her home."

Jay immediately throws off his white Chef hat, but keeps on his double-breasted Chef jacket, and rushes out front to greet Zamora. While she is glancing over the menu, he approaches unnoticed behind her.

"I HEARD the Filet Mignon with Mascarpone Mushroom Sauce is delicious."

Zamora turns around, smiling.

"Well, maybe I need to ask the chef to prepare that particular dish for me."

"He'll be delighted. Follow me." Jay leads her to the VIP section in his restaurant.

"Your restaurant is very nice."

"As is the way you look tonight."

A rosy glow of freshness appears on Zamora's face.

"I needed to get out; it's been a few days since I was able to do anything."

"I understand, please have a seat, Ms. Zamora, while I head to the kitchen to prepare our meal."

"Jay?"

"Yeah, what's up?"

"Thank you."

"No need to thank me; but you are welcome. In the meantime, would you like something to drink?"

"Jay, with the day I had yesterday, I'll just take a glass of water."

"One glass of water coming up."

Jay heads back to the kitchen to prepare their entrée. Alissa is their server for the night.

"Good evening, my name is Alissa. As requested, here is your water."

"Thank you."

"Wow, you smell very nice; may I ask the name of the perfume that you are wearing?"

"Oh, it's just something simple that I bought from Bloomingdales, it's "JOY" by Jean Patou."

"Girlfriend, that is nothing simple. I love that perfume; it is just so expensive. Well, it smells great with your body chemistry."

Jay approaches. "Alissa, are you bothering my guest as usual?"

Zamora says. "No bother at all, she couldn't be any more helpful."

"Now, Mr. Jay, why would I bother your company?"

"Because that is just what you do, Alissa," both are laughing.

"Whatever, Jay! Ma'am, thanks again for the information. I will leave you two alone; enjoy your meal." Then Alissa whispers in Jay's ears, "She's a doll."

"Girl, if you don't get back to work..." Jay says while laughing. Alissa heads back to the kitchen.

"The meal should be ready momentarily," Jay says to Zamora.

"Thank you, sit for a moment; keep me company for a bit.

"Give me fifteen; I'll be right back. But, before I head back to the kitchen, besides Jazz, what type of music do you listen to?

"Well, I pretty much like every genre of music, Robin Thicke, Guy, any old-school R&B, from R. Kelly to Marvin Gaye is gold with me."

"Alright, cool. I'll be back in a jiff."

Moments later a song plays "From the first time, I saw your face, girl I knew I had to have you. I wanted to grab you in…. Let's chill, let's settle down; that's what I want to do, just you and me." (Guy "Let's Chill")

Jay comes from around the corner, with a fork in his hand ad-libbing the song. Both hysterically laughing, while Cliff and Alissa bring on the meal.

"I love this song, Jay! Then again, who doesn't? Good choice." Zamora is completely flushed.

Jay walks over to Zamora, places the napkin on her lap. He moves back across the table to his seat.

"Enjoy!"

CHAPTER NINE
MORE QUESTIONS

"So, disclose information, Cliff, who is she? She is beautiful. And I see he went to the thick side." Alissa says.

"Yeah, well, the difference is she is *nicely* thick. You, on the other hand, ain't, Alissa!"

"Shut up, Cliff! Ugh, make me sick. So, what's the deal with them?"

"Why are you all up in his business? You want to fuck him?"

"Why must you be such an ass?! I just haven't seen him this happy in a while after the stunt his wife pulled; I hope she treats him well."

∽

"Jay, I am speechless! The meal was excellent. You really put your foot in this."

"Thank you, Zamora; that means a lot."

"Exceptional job, Jay, just exceptional."

"Have I told you how beautiful you look tonight?"

"Yes, you have."

"I am glad you stopped by."

"Jay, it's been weighing heavy on me, can we talk about what happened last night?"

"We really do not have to discuss it."

"I know, but I must. I was way beside myself; I'd endured so much in one day. I went to my sister's residence and gathered a few things. I came across her date book that she kept tons of personal things in. She talked about you a lot, and how you two would typically meet monthly at random hotels, how she loved being intimate with you; but as you said she didn't see it going anywhere because of your situation. But what bothers me the most is that you knew she was being abused."

Jay suddenly interrupts.

"Zamora, I didn't know exactly what was going on. Yes, I'd seen a few...."

"Jay, please, just allow me to finish. I need to get this off my chest. I am not upset that you knew, I mean, what were you to do? Call the police, and your wife would find out. She stated numerous times that you were her safe haven, so even during her rough times, you made her feel great, and that is all that matters to me. By the way, his name is Mike; he lives in Queens, and as you stated, she was very much in love with him and had full intentions of leaving Nazzir to be with him. I am just so shocked and appalled that my sister was doing all of this. She was always into respecting herself; I raised her so much better than that. Oh, to also add, I found another phone. I guess it's the phone she called me from on the night she was murdered. However, the phone is locked with a pass code that I can't seem to figure out."

"She said she was going to tell me everything, Jay; about you, Mike, and leaving her husband. Right before we got off the phone, that was the last time I heard from my sister."

"Maybe we can look for this Mike guy, who the heck he

is, where did they meet, does he even know that she's no longer with us? I don't know what to do; I just don't. I haven't been to work; this is my first meal in days. I am everywhere Jay, just in complete disarray. I can't thank you enough for being by my side."

Jay continues to stare at Zamora; their eyes were locked in a shared understanding during her conversation.

"I also called everyone and told them what happened and where the funeral will be held. I've decided to rest Zadie next to Momma and Poppa. Then the detective left a message; they caught him, Jay, they caught Nazzir. He is in bookings right now; I have so many questions to ask him; maybe, I should go see him."

Jay abruptly interrupted. "You will not go to see that monster, Zamora!"

"Jay, he killed my sister. He dumped her body, in some damn pit! Did he love her? He didn't love her! He couldn't love her! Why would he do something like that to someone he claims to love. It is not fair, Jay, this is just not fair! He took my sister from me; he took my lifeline! Did you know that she was pregnant?"

Jay's expression instantly flared up.

"Pregnant? No, she never told me."

"She was some time ago, but Nazzir killed my niece or nephew and may have killed my sister. We need to inform the detectives about this Mike guy. What if, think about it, what if Nazzir did not kill her. Not for anything; I am not trying to exclude him or bail him out. But who is this Mike guy? I must unlock her phone."

"So, as you can obviously see, this is a lot to take in; therefore, it explains why yesterday ended up the way it did." Zamora took a deep breath, covered her face with both hands in extreme shame.

"Jay, is any of this making sense to you?"

"It does Zamora; it makes complete sense."

He was lost for words. Not knowing what to say was a first for Jay. He needed time, time to think, and compress this all. Yet, at the same time, he doesn't want to leave Zamora in her thoughts.

"I have this guy that I can talk to who unlocks phones. I'll reach out to him tomorrow to see what he can do."

"That'll be so helpful, Jay."

"If there's anything I can do to help, I am there."

"You've helped so much, Jay, I don't know how else to thank you."

"Hey guys, is everything moving smoothly over here? Do you need me to take anything?" asks Alissa.

"Actually, yes, you can take everything and bring us another pitcher of water."

"Sure, Jay, no problem; would you guys like dessert?"

"Only if Jay makes it," Zamora states while smiling at Jay.

"Well, ma'am," says Alissa.

"Alissa, please call me Zamora."

"A beautiful name for a beautiful lady—and for the record, Ms. Zamora; Jay prepares desserts every morning. He makes the best cheesecake. Would you like to try it? I beg you to try."

"Sure, Alissa, I'll try it. Thank you."

"Two slices of caramel cheesecake on the way," as Alissa heads to the kitchen.

"She's a doll, Jay. She seems to have a crush on you."

"No, No, No, it's not me she has the crush on, hint, hint."

"Oh, stop it, Jay," Zamora says, laughing.

"She's like a little sister, a pain in the ass at times, but she's had a rough past. She's been incarcerated a few times, and yes, I did my due diligence prior. But I am willing to hire ex-cons that I see are willing to learn and build. Alissa went to culinary school, and 4 years later, she's one of my best cooks and hostesses; I don't regret it at all."

"You are a man of many surprises, Jay."

"So, this is the bitch that you've been ignoring my calls for?" Shrieks Teri as she wildly storms across the restaurant floor.

Jay shakes his head in dismay. "This can't be happening right now."

"Oh, you better believe that it is happening right now! Hi, I'm his wife, and you are?" Teri reaches out to shake Zamora's hand.

"A nobody, I am only a friend," Zamora says while looking directly at Jay.

"Were you aware that he's married?"

"Actually, yes, I am aware. But based on my recollection, he is seeking a divorce."

"But he is still married, bitch."

"Okay, that is the second time you called me a bitch; very mature of you."

"Teri, I am going to ask you one time to please leave my restaurant," Jay interrupts.

"Or what Jay, you'll physically throw me out? Why won't you just forgive me? Why are you out here doing me dirty like this? You know that I love you."

"You know what Jay, I'll just go," Zamora says rising from her chair.

"No! Zamora, you stay," commands Jay.

"Oh, so this bitch can stay, but I have to leave?"

"Teri, please just go!"

Teri becomes louder, causing more attention to the VIP section. By impulse, Jay stands up, grabs Teri by her arm, and herds her into his office.

During the commotion, Zamora runs to the bathroom, dries her tears then heads out of the restaurant. In the process, Alissa stops Zamora.

"You are too pretty to be crying, and if this helps, he is not into her anymore. I can see that you make him happy. Don't give up on him, especially because of this; she is just out of her mind."

"Thank you so much, Alissa. I am going through a lot right now. I just lost my sister, and I need some time. I am sure I'll see you around."

Forty-five minutes after Zamora departed from the restaurant, Jay realizes that she's gone. He's in distress, complete and utter disappointment.

"Cliff, give me a shot."

"I'm on it"…

"Here, Jay; man, I'm so sorry this shit happened."

Jay quickly threw back the shot of Hennessey.

"Thanks, Cliff, I have to run. I gotta make this shit right; she's burying her sister in a few days. She doesn't need this shit. Can you close up for me?"

"No doubt, Jay, I got you."

Jay heads to his car and proceeds to Zamora's home.

MAYBE I MADE it there before she did. Jay thought to himself, after noticing her car wasn't parked out front, nor has she answered any of his calls. Jay decides to wait for her arrival.

Jay's cell phone wakes him up. He then realizes he's been sitting outside her home for nearly two hours; still no sight of Zamora's car. He immediately proceeds to Cliff's house to stay the night, since his new place wouldn't be ready till the next few days. During his drive, he tries to reach Zamora again, to no answer.

While driving, Jay decides instead of going to Cliff's; he'll go to the Dumbo area instead, to clear his mind.

CHAPTER TEN

DUMBO REUNION

"It's a bit chilly out here," Jay says while placing his jacket over Zamora's shoulders.

"I must say this is the best sight in the entire area; not only due to the scenery, but because I've spotted you."

"Thank you; I am a bit chilly. How did you figure I'd be here?"

"Do you mind if I sit?"

"Please do." Jay sits down beside Zamora.

"Well, remember, you told me you come here just about every third day to clear your mind. I figured after waiting two hours for you at your home; you'd be here."

"I didn't know you'd go to my house. I am sorry."

"Before we get into anything, I just want to say I am sincerely sorry for what occurred tonight. She is a trip, but I didn't know she'd go this far."

"I accept your apology, but there is no need to apologize when you're in love and married, you'll do crazy things. I've been single for a while, but I do remember the feeling of being in love."

"Speaking of that, I've meant to ask: for a beautiful woman such as yourself, why are you single?"

"My ex was killed in a car accident. The one you did the repast for. Since then, I've been focused on myself; and I just haven't found the right man yet; I refuse to settle."

Jay understandably nods.

"Jay, I concluded that I am going to see Nazzir tomorrow. I must."

Jay sighs in dismay.

"Zamora, I just don't think it's a good idea. You're not emotionally stable enough to see him."

"I am sorry, Jay. But I truly need to do this, you must understand."

"As much as I don't agree, I can't stop you. But can I at least drive you?"

"That sounds like a good idea; how's tomorrow nine am?"

"I'll see you eight forty-five."

As Jay and Zamora, end the night by getting into their own cars, Zamora reaches out to one of Zadie's close friends, Shelly.

Shelly confirms that she remembers Zadie having an affair with a guy named Mike. Per Shelly, Zadie actually called him from Shelly's phone one night, when her phone died, to pick them up from a lounge.

Zamora asks Shelly to contact her phone service provider to try to obtain Mike's number. She wants to advise Mike of the situation, if he wasn't aware.

The Next Morning

Jay sits in his car in front of Zamora's home, waiting for her arrival. As Zamora walks out of her home towards his car, the day begins to move in slow motion; he is admiring Zamora's classy swayed approach, she is breathtaking.

"I can't thank you enough, Jay."

"You and your sister have the same toes."

"What?" Zamora says while laughing.

"I am going to call you *Jungletoes* from this day forward."

"Oh, no, you are not!"

"Put your seatbelt on Jungletoes."

Zamora jokingly hits Jay on his shoulders. "I can't believe you!"

"Get used to it; I plan on being around for a while." Zamora looks at Jay like all happiness was destined to just him.

"It seems we're thinking the same way."

BARBED WIRES

"Good Morning ma'am, have you been here before?" asks the officer.

"No, I haven't."

"Please fill out this visitation form."

Zamora is very uncomfortable visiting jail for the first time. There are tons of armed guards, locked doors, and tension.

The officer looks over her paperwork.

"Ms. Julius, do you by any chance know the inmate's Department Identification Number." (DIN)

"I am sorry, officer; but I do not have his DIN."

After waiting nearly forty-five minutes, the officer directs her to another security screening area that required her to empty her pockets, place her underwire bra in a brown paper bag then into the bin with her other items. Visitors walk through a security metal detector, are sniffed by dogs, then they are placed on a yellow charter school bus to the next area.

Barbed wire surrounds them, with cold concrete walls. She just can't wait to get out of here.

Upon getting off the bus, they are informed to provide their ID and the carbonless copy of the paperwork that they completed in the initial intake room. The officer then proceeds to guide the group of about twenty-seven people that exited the bus to another section of the jail. The officers advised the visitors to place their belonging, such as purses, and jackets, in their own personal lockers.

The group then enters another security screening, which leads them into a waiting area, where they call them in one by one, or in groups. She assumes that in the next room; they will finally be able to see the inmate. Zamora's name is called, her knees buckle. She is so scared and nervous.

She walks into another room where the other visitors are either talking or waiting for their loved ones to come out from behind the wall. Several minutes later, she sees him, Nazzir, the killer in question.

He reaches out to her, and an officer shouts, "No touching!" She pulls back.

"Don't touch me," she snarls at him with contempt in her eyes.

Nazzir takes a seat; they both seem obviously uncomfortable.

"I just want to know why?" Zamora asks.

"COME ON, SIS! You know I didn't kill my wife!"

"Don't you dare call me that!"

"I didn't do it! Yes, ok, we got into arguments. I abused her a few times, which was bad enough, but I would never kill your sister."

He begins to choke. As heartless as he is, seeing him weep made Zamora think differently. She has never seen Nazzir cry; she's known him for such a very long time, and this was the first.

"Sis, the spouse will always be the primary suspect. I am innocent until proven guilty. I have a great lawyer, and he will prove I am not the killer. What they need to be doing is looking for who really killed my fucking wife!"

As he slams his fists on the table, the guard rushes over and asks, "Is everything ok here?"

"Yes, officer, we are fine, sorry about that," says Zamora as the guard walks away.

"Do you think she was having an affair?"

"I *knew* she was, which is the main reason that we fought a lot. She started acting so differently, distancing herself. Things were never a hundred percent great with us, but I never cheated on my wife. Not to get overly personal, but we haven't been intimate in a very long time, and I was still faithful. I didn't care for anyone else.

"But whatever she was doing, with whomever she was doing it with, they need to question that person. You know I love your sister, I fell off, and I fucked up big time. I started to abuse my wife, and that was when shit got all fucked up; I am the one to blame. I put her out there; I put her in another man's arms. I got her killed; I got my wife killed! I should stay here for doing just that."

Zamora couldn't look away as she was hypnotized by his eyes.

"Do you know who she was having an affair with?"

"No, and I am glad I didn't find out, I would really be in here for murder. I don't need anything from you, Z; all that I need is for you to believe that I didn't do it and to find out who did!"

"Nazzir, I must go," Zamora states precipitously. "The funeral is tomorrow, and I have so much to do."

"Just find out who did it is all I ask, sis!"

Zamora practically runs out of the visiting room, thinking to herself, what if Jay killed her? She stops at the ladies' room to gather herself. She hears the toilet flush. A young lady walks towards the vanity.

She said, "It's rough, isn't it? Just hang in there, sister. My bae will be out in two years. I can't wait, enjoy your visit, sweetie."

"You too," she whispers. Zamora finally finds her way out of the prison; she holds her breath for a moment then exhales.

Zamora realized she leaves about thirty minutes to the time she told Jay to pick her up. She powers on her phone: her phone chimes--a text message from Shelly.

"Good morning, Zamora, is it Shelly. Here is Mike's number. I will see you at the funeral tomorrow. Again, I am so sorry for your loss."

Zamora replies: "Thank you very much, Shelly, I appreciate this. We will have repast at my house after the funeral; you are more than welcome to come.

Zamora dials the number provided; unfortunately, it went straight to voicemail. "Hello, this is Zamora,

Zadie's sister, I have some terrible news. Please return my call."

Zamora's phones chimes--a text message.

"I am sorry I missed your call; I am currently in a meeting; I will return your call momentarily-- auto reply message.

Reply text—"I apologize to bother you; my name is Zamora. I am Zadie's sister. Please return my call as soon as possible."

Jay arrives to pick her up.

"How did the visit go?" Jay asks Zamora as she climbs into the car.

"Shelly gave me Mike's number; I have his number, Jay," Zamora says with excitement. "I just called and left him a message."

As stern as Jay could sound, he asks again, "How did the visit go, Zamora."

"Naz told me to look at the person she was having the affair with!" Zamora states sarcastically.

Jay searches for answers in her eyes, but comes up empty.

"Hold up, are you implying that I had something to do with Zadie's death, Zamora?"

"Well, did you have something to do with it?"

"Get the fuck out of my car, Zamora," Jay states with extreme anger staring directly into Zamora's eyes.

Both sit silently; Zamora holds her breath, wanting to say something but she came up empty.

"I'll get out then!"

Jay storms out of his car, slams the door. Zamora follows behind him, yelling.

"Jay, stop, please, I am sorry, I didn't mean it! I don't know who to trust! Someone killed my baby sister! My mother and father are gone, now Zadie. I have nobody. Why can't you understand that everyone is a suspect? I don't know what to do anymore. I am so alone I just don't know what to do."

Zamora sits on the curb of the sidewalk, knees to her chest as she rocks back and forth, crying. Jay stares at her remorsefully and brimming with passion, he exhales and walks towards Zamora; he then kneeled beside her, now he sits astride with his legs over hers, arms around her waist. He whispers.

"You have me. I am sorry to have overreacted, but I need you to trust me when I say I don't have it in me to kill anyone, much less, your sister."

She rests her head on his shoulder. "I am sorry for accusing you."

He moves her hair to the side, places a gentle kiss on her neck, and then softly states, "Let's get out of here; you have a busy day."

Both enter the car and return to Zamora's home.

"Why don't you put your phone down? I am sure he will call you back."

"But what if he doesn't?"

Jay hands Zamora Zadie's unlocked phone.

"No way, you were able to unlock the phone, Jay?" She asks full of excitement.

"I am so scared to look through it."

"How about this; put the phone down, all of them, and let's prepare the meal for repast tomorrow."

"You are right; I will stop stressing out."

Jay and Zamora began to cook, with old school jamming in the background. Zamora made Zadie's three favorite dishes, Southern style black-eyed peas, buttermilk biscuits, and catfish po boys. All to be accompanied with braised collard greens, baked macaroni, and fried chicken.

Jay made jambalaya, red beans and rice, seafood gumbo, creamed corn, banana pudding, sweet potato pie, and caramel cheesecake.

The kitchen was in an uproar; six hours later, they were finally able to sit and relax for a bit.

"I am so sticky, I can't believe you seriously smothered me in caramel," Jay said jokingly.

"Oh, says the one who tried to pour flour all over my Gucci bag!"

"Stop it; it is just a bag."

"Just a bag, no sir, not just any bag—Dionysus GG bag; get it straight."

Jay grabs her purse from the couch; then he runs into the kitchen to get the bag of flour.

"Whoa, whoa, whoa! What are you doing?"

Jay walks tauntingly towards Zamora with the handbag in one hand and flour in the other.

"Omg Jay, what are you doing? No, please, put my bag down."

"Who's the man?"

"You, you, the man," she answers, giggling.

"What's my name?"

"What! Get out of here!"

"Don't make me ask again!"

"NO! *Jay*—that is your name!"

"Nope, wrong, try again!"

"What do you mean? How am I wrong? Jay is your name!" Zamora slowly walks towards Jay.

"No, no, no! You better stop it right there or else! Now, what's my name?"

"Ummm, wait, Jay, what is your last name, by the way?" Both busted out laughing.

"It's Jayden Carter, but don't change the subject!"

"Ok, ok, your name is Mr. Carter?"

"You are getting colder and colder Z, and this bag will look white in a few seconds."

"I got it!" Zamora yells. It's Mr. Jay Carter!"

"Wrong again, it's beginning to look a lot like Christmas over here."

"*Daddy*, is that it?"

"Ding ding ding! Yes, call me *Daddy* from now on, you got that?"

"Yes, I got it."

"Yes who?"

"Yes, Daddy, I got it!" Both are laughing at each other.

"Here, take your bg, cb, kb—whatever bag!"

"You play too much!" says Zamora, while snatching her bag from Jay. She immediately grabs her phone out of her bag to see if Mike texted or called.

"Anything from Mike," Jay asks.

"No, should I call him again?"

"Yeah, one more time for the night, Z, then that is it. I'll go take the last dish out of the oven."

"Hi Mike, it's Zamora again. Please give me a call back when you can."

Jay enters the room. "Did he answer this time?"

"No, he didn't." Jay sits beside Zamora on the couch while rubbing her shoulder.

"We'll figure this out together all right?"

"I know we will, Jay, thank you."

"Hey, how about this, I'll help you clean up the kitchen; then we'll call it a night so I can head back to Cliff's. I need a shower; I'm so sticky, thanks to you, knucklehead."

"You're more than welcome to stay if you want."

"I'd love to. However, I need to shower, and I don't have any clothes here. I can come over bright and early tomorrow."

"It is no burden if you want to stay. My guest room is always available."

Zamora has continually thought about Jay from the moment they met--everything reminds her of him. She often wonders if this is true love, infatuation, or vulnerability.

"How about this, I'll come back later tonight, after I clean myself up, if you don't mind?" Jay says.

"Well, I am sure I'll be sleeping, it is almost nine pm now. So, I will give you my keys. Just don't make any copies."

"I won't, Jungletoes. I'll see you shortly."

CHAPTER ELEVEN
JAY'S EPIPHANY

The moment Jay leaves, Zamora grabs Zadie's phone. After an hour goes by, she doesn't find anything incriminating or justifiable on Zadie's phone. It seems as if Zadie and Mike talked a lot, as they rarely ever texted. Then it dawned on her to check the voicemail.

"You have three new messages and two saved messages; press three to listen to new messages."

"A new message received Tuesday "Hey, Zadie, it's Mike. What the fuck did he do this time! Call me back, baby, please!"

"To save, press two; to skip the message, press the number sign. New message received Tuesday. "I received your urgent message; please give me a call-back baby. I am so sorry I missed you. Please return my call."

"To save, press two; to skip the message, press the number sign. New message received Tuesday, "I've called you twelve times. I need…Shit! you're calling back on the other end!" Mike clicked over to answer Zadie's incoming call.

This was the same night Zadie called her driving from the storage facility. Was he the last person to see her? Zamora ponders.

"To listen to saved messages, press six- you have two saved messages- 'Hi baby, it's Mike, let me know if we are meeting at the restaurant tonight and what time.' To re-save, press two, to skip the message, press the number sign; second, saved message. 'Hey baby, sorry I am late, I can't wait to see you. The restaurant is on the corner of 5th and Lexington, but I am parked on 8th walking towards you now.'"

Zamora's ringing phone startles her; she answers.

"Hey Jay"

"Z, are you doing okay?"

"Yes, I am doing fine."

"Did he get back to you yet?" Jay asks.

"I checked her messages. Mike spoke to Zadie the day she was killed. He called her a few times to no avail, then while he was in the process of leaving her a message, she called him back, and that was it; that was the last thing I heard."

"Hey Zamora, do me a favor and breathe," Jay says.

"I arrived at Cliff's; I'll see you in a few. You have a long day ahead of you tomorrow, put down the phones, and we will deal with this after the funeral, just not right now. Can you do that for me?

"Yes."

"Zamora, please."

"Okay, okay, I understand. Jay, I am sorry. I appreciate everything you did for me today with cooking and all; however, at this time, I feel it's best to be left alone tonight; and I will see you tomorrow at the funeral."

The ghostly silence on the other end of the phone clearly indicates that Jay is crushed.

"I'll see you tomorrow Zamora, have a good night," Jay disconnects the phone call.

Zamora runs to her room and drops onto her bed in distress. I miss you so much Zadie, what am I going to do without you? Zamora cries herself to sleep.

"MAN, Cliff, I know she is going through a lot, but she is giving me whiplash." As Jay and Cliff sit down to have a cold one, Cliff notices Jay's frustration.

"Aye Jay, don't fret. She'll come around. But I am having this badass shorty over tonight, she has a few friends, just say the word, and I got you. You lost someone dear to you too, and you haven't had the time to relax, and I mean relax."

"You know what; you're right, Cliff set that up!"

"Now, that's my man!"

About an hour later, Cliff and his lady friends entered the home. Music is playing; Jay is yet again in the kitchen cooking. This time he is only making artichoke spinach dip, crispy baked orange wings, chicken parmesan sliders and strawberry margaritas for the ladies. Ashe and Jay sip on some Cognac; the young lady walks into the living room, takes a seat near the window alongside her girlfriend.

"Wow, something smells great," the young lady states.

"My boy Jay is a chef; he owns the restaurant where I work." Jay comes out of the kitchen and notices two beautiful ladies.

Jay is fascinated by how beautiful his date looks. Her hair is midnight black and it flowed over her shoulders. She has a thin comely sculpted figure with a beautiful dark complexion. Her clothing is simple, black fitted pencil skirt, with what seems to be a blue and gray crew-neck bodysuit, with crop earrings.

"Jay, this is Joanne. Joanne, this is my best friend Jay," says Cliff.

"Hi, Jay, it's a pleasure to meet you."

"The pleasure is mine, would you ladies like something to eat or drink?" Jay asks.

"Sure, I'll take both. Do you need help in the kitchen?" asks Joanne.

"Actually, I wouldn't mind the help at all." Both walk into the kitchen.

"So, you too are a chef, huh?"

"Yes, and what about you, what do you do?"

"I am a dancer."

"Go figure, I can tell by your amazing figure. You are certainly built to be one. What is that you do, ballet?"

"No, actually, I am an Exotic Dancer."

"Oh," Jay holds his breath in shock.

"Oh, wow, that explains your beautiful figure even more." They both laughed.

"Excuse me for a moment." Jay walks into the living room where Cliff and his date were close in an affectionate manner.

"Cliff, can you meet me in the backroom for a second?" As they walk into the room, Jay closes the door behind them.

"A fucking stripper, Cliff?"

"What the fuck are you tripping for, you trying to wife the bitch? Come on, man, you are tripping right now, I'm going back to my date!"

"You still don't understand me, do you? This isn't me, Cliff! I am not living this life anymore; I have no time to even be with fucking broads of this reputation."

"Have fun with her; think outside the box sometimes! You sound gay, my man, I am out." Cliff storms out of the room.

Joanne asked, "Hey, is everything okay?"

"Yes, we are good, Queen. I need to head out to my car to grab my phone; I'll be right back. Go get yourself something to drink."

Jay gets into his car, places his head on the headrest. His phone chimes; he receives a text message.

"Hey, Jay, it's Zamora. Yet again, I overreacted; I apologize. You can come by if you want. The guest room is unlocked with sheets on the bed. I will see you soon. Drive safe."

Even though Zamora's message was sent nearly two hours ago, without hesitation, Jay starts his car and heads to Zamora's home.

Jay arrives at Zamora's, and he enters the kitchen to make sure all dishes were placed in the fridge, grabs a bottle of water, turns off all lights, and then heads upstairs to the guest room. In passing Zamora's room, she seems to be peacefully sleeping. He closes her door.

Jay enters the guest room, prepared the sheets for the bed, turns on the bedside radio, and then lies down in deep thought.

Moments later, he finds himself standing in front of Zamora's bedroom door.

ABOUT THE AUTHOR

T. Xorí Williams was born in Brooklyn, New York City. Xorí began writing woman inspirational quotes to friends and family, who often asked: "When are you going to write a book?"
She finally wrote her own novel, inspired by the Sister Souljah, Teri Woods, Donald Goines, Zane, James Patterson, Nora Roberts, *Twilight*, and the E. L. James series.
While working two jobs, and still attending school, Xorí began writing, completing her first manuscript in 2017. Xorí has developed an ability to alter many projects at once, researching one book while outlining another. Xorí then decided to self-publish her first novel online. From an early age, she always dreamed of writing stories that readers will fall in love with, and that dream has come true.

Facebook - https://www.facebook.com/txoriwilliams
Instagram - https://www.instagram.com/txoriwilliams/

ISBN: 9781973925644

A NOTE FROM THE AUTHOR

Thank you for reading *Co-Incidental Encounters, Unbearable; Book One.* I hope you enjoyed reading it as much as I enjoyed writing it.

Be sure to watch for the second book of this series where you will find the answers to all of your questions about Zamora, Jay, and whodunit!

Made in the USA
Middletown, DE
06 June 2022

66752147R00086